Standards and Guidelines for

ADULT DAY CARE

Prepared by
The National Institute on Adult Daycare
a constituent unit of
The National Council on the Aging, Inc.

As approved by
The NIAD Delegate Council

As adopted by
The NCOA Board of Directors April 1990

Made possible by a grant from the Vira I. Heinz Endowment

Published by The National Council on the Aging, Inc.
600 Maryland Avenue, SW, West Wing 100
Washington, DC 20024

Standards and Guidelines for Adult Day Care is a new edition, revised and
expanded, of the *Standards for Adult Day Care*, originally published in 1984.
Second edition, 1990.
Printed in the United States of America.
1990, 2K

Library of Congress Cataloging-in-Publication Data

National Institute on Adult Daycare (U.S.)
      Standards and guidelines for adult day care / prepared by the National
Institute on Adult Daycare, a constituent unit of The National Council on
the Aging, Inc.
      244p. 21.5cm.
      "As approved by the NIAD Delegate Council, as adopted by the
NCOA Board of Directors, April 1990."
      Rev. and expanded ed. of: Standards for adult day care, 1984.
      Includes bibliographical references.

      ISBN 0-910883-54-8

      1. Day care centers for the aged—Standards—United States.
I. National Council on the Aging. II. National Institute on Adult Daycare
(U.S.) Standards for Adult. III. Title.
      [DNLM: 1. Day Care—in old age. 2. Day Care—standards—United
States. 3. Health Services for the Aged—organization & administration
United States. WT 29 AA1 B27s]
HV1461.N364 1990
363.6'3—dc20   90-13518
                                         CIP

● ii

This document is dedicated to the men and women served in adult day care programs, now, in the past, and in the future, and to their families and caregivers.

We thank the following photographers and agencies for their contributions appearing on the pages noted:

Thomas Hardin and West Haven Adult Day Center
(pages 10, 17, 69, 102, 129)

Sven Martinson and Connecticut Community Care, Inc. (page 1)

Tom Reese and *Seattle Times* (page 84)

Ralph Ricketts and
Clayton County (Georgia) Alzheimer's Day Center (page 109)

On Lok Senior Health Services (page 37)

Seattle Day Center for Adults (page 211)

The effort to produce this document
and the companion document,
*Standards and Guidelines for Adult Day Care:
A Self-Assessment Workbook*
was made possible by the generous support of the
Vira I. Heinz Endowment, Pittsburgh, Pennsylvania.

The National Council on the Aging, Inc. and
the National Institute on Adult Daycare
are most grateful to the Endowment for its funding
and for the support of, and commitment to, the project.

Adult Day Care: A Definition

Adult day care is a community-based group program designed to meet the needs of adults with functional impairments through an individual plan of care. It is a structured, comprehensive program that provides a variety of health, social, and related support services in a protective setting during any part of a day but less than 24-hour care.

Individuals who participate in adult day care attend on a planned basis during specified hours. Adult day care assists its participants to remain in the community, enabling families and other caregivers to continue caring at home for a family member with an impairment.

Contents

Special Subcommittee on Guidelines for Programs
Serving Individuals with Alzheimer's Disease and
Other Dementias 215

Preface

by Mary Ann Outwater

Chair, National Institute on Adult Daycare (NIAD), 1990-1992
Chair, National Institute on Adult Daycare (NIAD)
Standards and Guidelines Committee, 1984-1990

Since the National Institute on Adult Daycare (NIAD) developed the first set of national standards for adult day care in 1984, the field has changed dramatically. You will read about its growth and expansion in the introduction to the Standards and Guidelines section of this document. You will read about the changes in its services and focus, and learn more about its expansion, in the Philosophy section. And, in both sections, you will learn about the all-important changes in the participants served in adult day care since 1984. However, there is another change just as important. This is the significant movement toward increased professionalism in the field of adult day care.

As this relatively young service matures, the changes instituted by you, the providers, in response to your day center participants are the changes that we have tried to capture and incorporate in these 1990 standards. You have made great strides in professionalizing this service, and we have attempted to restate the best of your accomplishments to serve as guidelines for practice from which others can benefit. These standards are reflective of the field and designed to meet the needs of practitioners who, in turn, must meet the needs of participants.

 Adult day care is now recognized as a viable quality service within the continuum of long-term care in the United States. NIAD has, from its inception, worked not only to increase the visibility of adult day care but also has dedicated itself to the development and implementation of quality service. The continuous input of providers, and of regulators, has enabled us to keep abreast of current knowledge and of the many factors that have direct impact on service delivery.

Adult day care is a grassroots movement. Similarly, the ongoing standards and guidelines development is a grassroots process: practitioners communicating from the program level to the state level, to the national level— always seeking more effective ways to meet the needs of participants.

The 1984 standards were developed as part of an ongoing process. These 1990 standards are another step in that process. We expect this process to continue—with your help.

A critical component of the process used in developing the standards was the solicitation of responses to the first complete draft of the standards from more than 500 providers, state associations of providers, and state monitoring agencies. The input was invaluable, giving us much direction in refining the standards.

This document reflects many years of work and diligent input of practitioners from all parts of the country under the leadership of a dedicated NIAD Standards and Guidelines Committee and Task Force on Standards. The 1984 standards provided an excellent foundation for this 1990 revision. Current trends and needs led the NIAD leaders to include separate guidelines for programs caring for persons with dementia, as well as profiles of specialized programs. These areas are included to assist practitioners as the new specialty programs and programming evolve. The *Self-Assessment Workbook* is a response to requests by providers for a working document to assist them in the implementation of standards and guidelines.

Through the generosity of the Vira I. Heinz Endowment, this project has been directed by Mary Brugger Murphy. To both we are extremely grateful. To the Endowment and to project officers Dana Phillips and Carole Parker, we express thanks for their support and encouragement. To Mary, we thank you for your dedication, your never ending professionalism, your ability to take the reams of input from providers, state associations, and agencies and fashion it into a collective document to be reviewed, discussed, and revised by the Task Force and Delegate Council—time and time again, until this final presentation—and for your sense of humor and friendship.

This document is the effort of many people: practitioners, family members, and the talented and generous staff of The National Council on the Aging. We thank the NCOA Board of Directors and NCOA President Dr. Daniel Thursz; we particularly thank Tammy Clark, Louise Cleveland, Tanya Hart, Dorothy Howe, Bill Oriol, and Brenda Robinson for their commitment and contributions.

It is expected that these Standards and Guidelines will demonstrate their validity as they are disseminated and implemented. It is also expected that these standards will expand and change as the field continues to develop. Providers are encouraged to share information on the needs of day care participants and caregivers, as well as efforts in program development, on a state and national level. Providers must continue to apprise the NIAD Delegate Council and Standards Committee of developments in the field, so that the national Standards and Guidelines for Adult Day Care can continue to ensure the delivery of quality care to day care participants and their families.

● x

Philosophy

In the past, the adult day care field has struggled with the concept of classifying programs based on models of care. This concept had its origins in early European programs where adult day care was defined according to the treatment emphasis such as social work, psychiatry, or physical therapy. Throughout the United States, program development based on specific models has continued, often reinforced by regulatory agencies, funding sources, and parent organizations.

In 1984 practitioners in the field saw a rapid development of programs without a clear definition of the services. In response, The National Institute on Adult Daycare (NIAD) took the position that the national standards to be developed that year should be generic standards and guidelines for quality care and good practice, regardless of focus, sponsoring organization, or funding sources. The standards were intended to:

- assist and encourage development of new centers;

- improve the quality and efficiency of existing centers; and

- provide national direction for policy formation.

In developing the 1984 standards, models that differentiated programs on the basis of health and non-health services were eliminated. Instead, emphasis was placed on encouraging the development of diverse programs that could be expanded or modified as dictated by the needs of the population served.

The 1984 standards became the basis for many state

regulations. Unfortunately, however, state licensing and certification standards often failed to recognize the central concept—that adult day care is not a static program but rather a program that is dedicated to meeting the needs of the population served. This means that if needs change, often so do centers. The extent of the changes is influenced by center resources, facility limitations, governmental requirements, availability of qualified staff, and other community services.

In this 1990 revision of the national adult day care standards, the generic position has been maintained. Providers have found that today's adult day care population is older and more frail, and has more impairments, a greater incidence of Alzheimer's disease, and more complex health care needs.

The findings of the 1985-86 NIAD National Adult Day Care Survey raised the question of the validity of the "social" and "health" models. For example, findings showed that staff nursing services were provided by 571 day care centers (70 percent of the centers responding). However, only 280 centers were licensed for health care and only 165 centers (28 percent) received Medicaid funding.

An in-depth analysis of the 1985-86 survey data was conducted in an attempt to provide answers to the many questions raised by survey findings. The report, *Adult Day Care: A Program of Services for the Functionally Impaired*, 1988, presents the results of the analysis. The predominant research question used in this analysis was intended to categorize, if possible, day care centers by program and participant characteristics in order to increase the understanding of how and why day care centers differ. Questions were raised regarding the relationships that may exist between licensing categories, funding sources, and participant and center characteristics.

These were among the major findings:

- Licensing category and major funding source account for only a small percentage of the differences in service packages, some participant characteristics, and costs of adult day care centers.

- Participant sub-groups (persons with developmental disabilities; persons who are wheelchair bound; persons living with family, relatives, or friends; and persons living alone) were found in all centers regardless of funding source or licensing category.

The report reached this conclusion:
"Adult day care is a growing evolving program. Dedicated to meeting participants' needs, developed without external influences in many cases, the parameters, the services, the philosophy, the participants all form an identifiable group. It is a program providing a range of services in a structured, centralized setting, designed to meet the restorative and maintenance needs of functionally impaired individuals and their families. The configuration of a particular center at a given point in time reflects perceived needs and center ability to meet these needs. Ideally, as needs change, so does the program—adding new services, trying different techniques and emphases. However, the ability to make changes to meet all needs means, in many centers, an increase in their resources."

The 1989 National Adult Day Center Census, which identified approximately 2,100 centers and received information from 84 percent of those, also found a strong common core of services and a common target population.

*The number of centers that provided health services—
nursing services (964), physical therapy (752),
occupational therapy (721), speech therapy (684) and
medical assessment (711)—is greater than the number of
centers that received funds from a health funding source
(518) or had a health-related license (615).*

*Over three-quarters of the centers serve persons with
Alzheimer's disease, visual and hearing impairments,
physical handicaps, mental retardation and developmental
disabilities, persons in wheelchairs needing assistance in
transferring, and the aged. Seventy percent serve persons
with frequent (more than weekly) incontinence. Fifty-six
percent of all participants across all centers need
assistance or are dependent in two or more activities of
daily living (ADLs). Faced with such findings and the
experiential knowledge of its members, NIAD has rejected
the idea of discrete models perpetuated by a long-standing
tradition of separation of social and health services in state
licensing agencies and state/federal funding sources.*

*The surveys reported the reality of adult day care—not
the theoretical models postulated by regulation. Clearly
centers often go beyond what is required in their efforts to
meet changing needs.*

The 1990 standards repeatedly state that adult day care
centers must follow state requirements. These must take
precedence over voluntary national standards.

In the standards the emphasis is on meeting the needs of
participants served. If a participant has needs the center
cannot meet, there are several options available.

1. Do not accept the participant. Eligibility criteria
should address specifically the needs a center can and
cannot meet.

2. If the participant is already in the program but a
change has taken place, the center may:

- discharge the participant and assist in transfer to a more appropriate service;

- arrange for the need to be met by community resources; or

- modify the facility or add the appropriate staff and/or equipment to meet the need.

Survey findings indicate many centers have chosen this last option.

The 1990 standards are written in such a way that centers that now consider themselves "social," that is providing no health-related service, can meet the service requirements. The Nursing Services specified in Standard 62 (Part Three: Services) can be carried out by non-nursing staff, with a nurse consultant providing direction for a few hours monthly. If this is the center's choice, then their eligibility criteria should reject persons who require the constant availability of a professional nurse.

For those centers that do provide any of the health-related services, standards are stated for that purpose. It is the center's decision.

The NIAD standards of 1984 had enormous influence on state standard development. The standards of 1990 reflect the reality and point the way for government regulatory agencies. It is time to reject artificial "levels of care" and health/social separation and to recognize adult day care as a continuum of care—stretching from limited direct services to intensive and extensive medical and therapeutic services. It is also important to recognize that the population served is not static—needs can change rapidly. Each day care center needs to decide how to handle the changing needs of the participants served.

NIAD recommends that state and federal regulatory

agencies consider the development of a generic licensing category for all adult day care centers, based on the 1990 standards. Funding sources may continue to specify characteristics of persons eligible for their reimbursement. With this arrangement, a center may continue to serve the participants funded by a variety of sources and may adjust their service package when indicated by participant needs, without needing another license. The center would specify the essential services, any of the other services, and their eligibility criteria in their applications for initial and renewal licensure.

Such a generic license would allow day centers to develop participant-centered programs that are responsive to the wide and ever-changing range of abilities, limitations, and needs found among the participants in adult day care centers.

In the meantime, NIAD offers its 1990 standards, designed to reflect the commonalities and interdependence among all components of an effective adult day care program and to respond to the need for flexibility. The intent of these revised standards is to allow the development of programs that respond to participant needs rather than focus on reimbursement sources, cost of service, or staffing levels. These standards, as those developed in 1984, should be used as a tool for fostering quality programs that are effective and responsive and that meet the needs of adults with functional impairments.

Statement of Rights of Adult Day Care Participants

The following is a statement of rights of persons enrolled in adult day care programs. Though the statement is not intended to be inclusive, it suggests an outline of the basic tenets that should be followed in providing day care services for adults.

- The right to be treated as an adult, with consideration, respect, and dignity, including privacy in treatment and in care for personal needs.

- The right to participate in a program of services and activities designed to encourage independence, learning, growth, and awareness of constructive ways to develop one's interests and talents.

- The right to self-determination within the day care setting, including the opportunity to:
  - participate in developing one's plan for services and any changes therein
  - decide whether or not to participate in any given activity
  - be involved to the extent possible in program planning and operation
  - refuse treatment and be informed of the consequences of such refusal
  - end participation in the adult day care center at any time.

- The right to be cared about in an atmosphere of sincere interest and concern in which needed support and services are provided.

- The right to a safe, secure, and clean environment.

- The right to confidentiality and the requirement for written consent for release of information to persons not authorized under law to receive it.

- The right to voice grievances without discrimination or reprisal with respect to care or treatment that is (or is not) provided.

- The right to be fully informed, as evidenced by the participant's written acknowledgment of these rights, of all rules and regulations regarding participant conduct and responsibilities.

- The right to be free from harm, including unnecessary physical or chemical restraint, isolation, excessive medication, abuse, or neglect.

- The right to be fully informed, at the time of acceptance into the program, of services and activities available and related charges.

- The right to communicate with others and be understood by them to the extent of the participant's capability.

Intent

These Standards and Guidelines are intended as descriptions of outstanding efforts currently underway and goals for which to strive in the growing field of adult day care. They are national, voluntary standards. They are superseded by existing state and local laws and regulations.

If a state government is interested in modifying its standards or developing new standards, these standards will offer guidance and direction; however, they must be appropriately tailored to the population, programs, needs, resources, and unique characteristics in the state.

These standards define programs that are participant-centered. In order to be used appropriately, they must be applied and evaluated with sufficient flexibility to allow maximum responsiveness to participants and to their changing needs.

The Adult Day Care Center Standards and Guidelines

Introduction

In 1984 the National Council on the Aging's National Institute on Adult Day Care (NCOA/NIAD) promulgated national standards for adult day care. The standards presented a broad consensus on quality adult day care at that time. They were developed by a group of providers representing a range of approaches to adult day care and also reflected the input of the many providers, associations, and agencies with which they were shared as proposed standards.

Since then, the ongoing evolution of service delivery to both older persons with impairments and younger disabled adults, the development of specialized programs (such as those for individuals with dementia), and the rapid emergence of numerous adult day care centers have necessitated the revision of the national standards.

Further, in 1986, when NIAD's Standards Committee completed a survey of persons who used the standards, 72 percent of the respondents agreed that a self-assessment workbook should accompany the standards. Such a workbook, it was felt, would enable programs nationwide to assess quality, evaluate their growth, and plan future direction.

In 1988 NCOA/NIAD developed a proposal to upgrade and update its national standards, add standards for programs serving persons with dementia, address programs that serve other specialized populations, and develop a self-assessment instrument to enable adult day care programs to improve their own operations.

The proposal was submitted to and, in November 1988, was funded by, the Vira I. Heinz Endowment in Pittsburgh,

Pennsylvania. During the following eighteen months the work was completed through the efforts of the NIAD Task Force on Standards and the many other individuals identified in this volume.

The result is this 1990 *Standards and Guidelines for Adult Day Care* and the accompanying self-assessment tool, *Standards and Guidelines for Adult Day Care: A Self-Assessment Workbook.*

Minimal, or High Quality?

The goal of this effort is to strengthen programs for adults with functional impairments by developing and promulgating national standards that define a program of high quality for adult day care centers.

A conscious decision was made to describe goals that reflect a high quality of care rather than minimal requirements and that offer an ideal for centers to strive for. Since an important function of NCOA/NIAD is to provide leadership and direction in this field, this opportunity was used to define measurable criteria for assuring quality. Many fine programs, offering sound services, will not be in a position to meet all of these standards. Centers will, however, have clear guidance on the direction in which programs should move as they evolve, mature, and serve an increasingly impaired population. It is anticipated that as more of these standards are achieved by a center, the program will be strengthened. That is the primary goal.

In applying the standards to a particular center, three considerations are key:

● Defining the target populations to be served is a critical starting point.

● Providing the scope and intensity of services and level of staffing needed to serve that population is the underlying purpose.

● Flexibility in applying the standards, and modification when necessary and appropriate, is essential to that purpose.

The standards were written with the intent of producing a participant-centered program responsive to the wide (and ever-changing) range of abilities, limitations, and needs found among the participants in almost all adult day care centers.

Steady Growth, New Demands

It was noted in the 1984 standards publication that "the past decade has seen a dramatic growth in the number of adult day care programs in the United States, from less than a dozen in the early 1970s to more than a thousand centers today." Based upon a survey conducted recently by the University of California-San Francisco, and facilitated by NCOA/NIAD, it can be added that the most recent six years have witnessed even more dramatic growth. There are now at least twenty-one hundred (2,100) adult day care centers. (It should be noted that more centers serving non-elderly participants with developmental disabilities and mental illness were identified in this recent survey.) Available evidence also demonstrates an increase in the total numbers of persons being served in day centers, reflecting growth in day care and an increased need.

At least as significant is the change in the population being served in adult day care centers. The anecdotal information offered by adult day care center staff members who have been in the field for the last ten to fifteen to twenty years clearly indicates a marked increase in the acuity level of most participants. The population generally is older, more frail, more impaired, has a greater incidence of Alzheimer's disease, and has more complex health care needs. Further, centers that have maintained their participant files over a period of years have found that there is documentation of a significant increase in impairment level. For example, in one center in Northern Virginia it was observed that: in 1981, 49% of those enrolled suffered from dementia—by 1988, that had increased to 70% (and with more severe impairment than in 1981); in 1981, 5% of the participants wandered from the center—in 1988, 47% were wanderers; and in 1981, 5% were wheelchair bound and 8% needed help walking—in 1988 12% were in wheelchairs and 51% in need of a staff member's help to walk.

Two Key Principles

The twenty-one hundred adult day care centers—like the hundreds of thousands of participants served—have as many differences from one another as similarities. On two important points, however, there are essential commonalities. The first is the **interdisciplinary functioning of the staff**. It is universally found in adult day care centers that programs are strengthened and services improved when the participants' needs take precedence over rigid or artificial lines of responsibility. Because the program is client-centered and since the participants' needs are complex and inter-related, staff interaction and collaboration are needed to respond to those needs.

The second common element in adult day care is the **therapeutic milieu**. All that occurs in the center takes place for the purpose of improving the quality of life of the participant. Throughout the day, all actions and words center on participants' needs and the improvement of their well being.

The setting of an adult day care program offers, first of all, a pleasant and enjoyable environment. There is music, conversation, activity, and much more. This setting by itself is actually therapeutic. It is within this environment that all of the various disciplines do their work, for example, nursing, social work, therapies, and dietetics. The participants become part of a dynamic environment that adds a measure of satisfaction, involvement, and pleasant anticipation to their lives.

The unique blend of characteristics of the adult day care center, as a mode of service delivery, includes: a primary focus on the holistic needs of the participant, the individualized plan of care for each participant, the significance of the family or caregiver and consideration of their needs, and the importance of the sense of community — the sense of belonging that alleviates the isolation caused by the severe impairments experienced by the participants.

After a participant spends a few sessions in adult day care, comments from families often reflect the participant's change in attitude, new interest in life, and, for the cognitively intact, renewed motivation to work toward his or her highest level of functioning. The therapeutic strength of adult day care lies in the blend of a structured health oriented program with a relaxed environment.

A Continuum of Care

Programs and populations vary — and they change daily with changes in functional levels of participants. Adult day care centers must be prepared to respond to a wide range of participant needs. Centers whose participants currently may not need extensive medical and therapeutic services will most likely at some point in the future find that they require the additional services — and the center will need to provide them.

Adult day care programs are accurately described along a continuum of care — stretching from limited direct services to intensive and extensive medical and therapeutic services. These standards are intended to describe a foundation of quality care appropriate for all types of adult day care programs.

Program Flexibility

The standards presented here define a program of high quality and offer goals for which to strive. The application of the standards requires the balance provided by appropriate flexibility. NIAD offers the following **statement on flexibility**, intended to protect evolving programs, encourage innovation, and lead to consideration of acceptable modifications that permit programs to grow while continuing to provide appropriate care to participants:

> NIAD recognizes the variety and richness of adult day care programs. Developing standards that are appropriate for all programs is difficult. It is not possible to

foresee all the various circumstances that may occur. Therefore, NIAD recommends that state licensing, certifying, funding, accrediting, and/or monitoring agencies incorporate into their laws, regulations, policies, and guidelines the authority to grant program flexibility.

Program flexibility means the approval of alternative ways to meet the intent of a standard so long as safe and quality care is provided. Alternatives may include concepts, methods, procedures, techniques, equipment, personnel qualifications, and facility requirements. The governing state agency (usually the licensing and/or reimbursement agent) should have authority to override specific requirements in law, regulations, policies, and procedures if, in its judgment, the intent of the requirement is met by the proposed alternative, and safe and quality care will be provided.

When a program director suggests an alternative to a state requirement, a written request—specifying what law, procedure, policy, or regulation would be waived and describing how the applicant proposes to meet the intent of the requirement—should be submitted to the appropriate state agency(s) for prior approval before the proposed alternative is implemented. An approval period may be time-limited or indefinite, depending on the nature of the request.

An example of program flexibility is the opportunity to retain effective staff members who do not meet the credentials recommended. It is recognized that there are many fine staff members with many years of experience in adult day care who are capable of providing excellent care. The standards are not designed to suggest removing them from their positions. Rather, the standards seek to protect future programs against detrimental hiring practices and offer an indicator of quality to others. Specifically, in this use of flexibility, if a center has made diligent efforts to recruit appropriate personnel, without success, and if a waiver of requirements (particularly educational requirements) will not endanger the health or safety of participants, then such a waiver may be sought.

Federal, State, and Local Requirements

It is essential that these standards be considered at all times with the understanding that federal, state, and local laws, ordinances, regulations, and requirements *always take precedence over these recommended, voluntary standards.*

Part One:
Target Population*

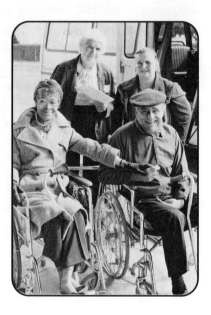

1 **Each center shall define the target populations it is able to serve, considering the needs of the participants and availability, frequency, and intensity of services.**

As adult day care is an evolving program, external and internal influences are subject to change. The target population will vary within each setting depending upon community needs; licensing and funding requirements; the

---

*NOTE: Standards are numbered and in bold; recommendations are italicized.

center's assessment of participants' needs, space, and staff; and the parent oganization's philosophy and mission. Target populations may change, depending on need; and services will need to change. Services offered must meet the needs of participants. The configuration of a particular center at a given point in time reflects these influences.

A guiding principle for all adult day care centers is neither to admit knowingly nor to continue caring for participants whose needs cannot be met by the program directly or in cooperation with outside resources. Therefore:

> **2** **Adult day care centers shall not serve participants whose needs exceed resources or those served more appropriately in a less structured setting.**

> **3** **In determining an appropriate target population, adult day care centers shall consider not only the scope of services they will be providing but also the level of service intensity.**

In determining appropriateness, the needs of a participant and the frequency and intensity of services available to meet these needs are to be considered.

For example, there is a definite distinction between offering regular blood pressure and weight checks and offering daily nursing services ranging from skilled nursing to supportive and personal care. Further, consultants such as physical therapists or occupational therapists may provide assistance in developing a general exercise program, *or* they may do assessments, care planning, provision of skilled rehabilitation services, and supervision of maintenance therapy.

---

4 **Individuals eligible for adult day care shall include:**

● **those who have physical, cognitive, and/or psycho-social impairments**

● **those capable of being transported**

● **those capable of benefiting from socialization, structured/supervised programs, or group-oriented programs.**

Possible Target Populations

The population served will vary according to the identified need of the community and the goals, resources, and capability of the organization providing the service. The target population includes one or more of the following groups of individuals.

Adults with physical, psycho-social, or mental impairments who require assistance and supervision, such as:

● persons who have few or inadequate support systems

● persons who require assistance with activities of daily living (ADLs) and instrumental activities of daily living (IADLs)

● persons with physical problems that require health monitoring and supervision on a regular basis

● persons with emotional problems that interfere with one's ability to cope on a daily basis

● persons with memory loss and cognitive impairment that interfere with daily functioning

● persons with developmental disabilities

● persons who require assistance in overcoming the isolation associated with functional limitations or disabilities

● persons whose family and/or caregiver needs respite care.

Adults who need rehabilitative services (including restorative and maintenance) in order to restore or maintain the optimum level of functioning, such as:

● persons recently discharged from hospitals or nursing homes

● persons needing therapy, due to some chronic disability, to adjust to their limitations and learn adaptive skills

● persons who, without program intervention, are at risk of premature institutionalization due to physical deterioration or their psychological condition

● persons who need support in making the transition from independent living to group care or in making the transition from group care to independent living.

Adults who require services provided by or under the supervision of a licensed nurse (Registered Nurse, Licensed Practical Nurse, or Licensed Vocational Nurse) in accordance with federal and state requirements, such as:

● assessment

● supervision or administration of medications and observation of their effects

● treatments

● health education and training in self care

● training in activities of daily living (ADLs)

● assistance in ADLs.

Determining an Appropriate Target Population

5 **All adult day care centers shall have a written policy on participants who are appropriate and those who may not be appropriate for enrollment.**

The appropriate target population will vary within each setting, depending on community needs, staffing, and service availability. Generally, those who may not be appropriate for enrollment include adults whose need for care requires staff time and skills different from those the individual program is able and qualified to provide as well as adults who can function in a less structured setting.

It is the responsibility of each center, as noted earlier, to define the target population it is able to serve, considering the needs of the participant and the frequency and intensity of services. The availability of professional and paraprofessional services will enable the center to serve participants with added needs.

For Example:

Participants appropriate for centers with professional nursing services available when participants are present include adults who cannot self-administer medications required during hours at the center (unless another person licensed or certified by the state such as a medication aide or psychiatric technician is on staff and present).

Participants appropriate for centers that have available a physical or occupational therapist or speech pathologist or the ability to arrange for these specialists include adults who will benefit from skilled therapy services as ordered by the physician.

Participants who are inappropriate for all adult day care centers include:

● Adults who are bedfast or do not have the strength or the stamina to attend adult day care for the minimum required hours as defined in state licensing requirements.

● Adults in an infectious stage of a communicable disease unless a physician states there is no significant hazard. (They shall only be admitted under guidance of the health department and/or licensing authority.) This is intended to protect the health of the center participants and is not intended to discriminate against any individual.

● Adults with emotional or behavioral disorders who are destructive to self or others or disruptive in a group setting—unless the center has the capacity, including qualified staff, to adequately and appropriately manage these problems.

● Adults who are actively alcoholic or addicted to drugs—unless the center has the capacity, including qualified staff, to adequately and appropriately manage these problems.

● Adults who are too independent to benefit from the activities and services provided in the adult day care center, and who need referral to other more appropriate programs such as a senior center or nutrition site.

Part Two: Administration and Organization*

The Governing Body

6 Unless the center is independently owned or functions through a governmental unit, a formal governing body shall have full legal authority and fiduciary responsibility for the operation of the program, adopting bylaws and rules that address:

● **purposes of the program**

● **governing body's composition and size, and members' and committee chairs' terms of office**

● **frequency of meetings.**

---

*NOTE: Standards are numbered and in bold; recommendations are italicized.

When the adult day care center is a subdivision or subunit of a multifunction organization, the governing body of the multifunction organization may serve as the governing authority of the adult day care center.

Responsibilities of the governing body include:

● determining the center's program and operating policies

● developing an organizational structure that defines lines of authority to implement the program and policies

● appointing and evaluating and/or approving the appointment of a qualified administrator

● determining the scope and quality of services provided to participants and families/caregivers in response to defined need (See Part One: Target Population)

● establishing an advisory committee

● reviewing and overseeing the center's fiscal affairs, including adopting an annual budget, setting fees, and managing of financial risk

● arranging for an annual program and financial audit

● developing long-range plans

● conducting evaluations

● ensuring the program's continual compliance and conformity with all relevant federal, state, local, or municipal laws and/or regulations that govern operation of adult day care facilities

● approving written agreements and collaborative relations with other agencies for specified services

● approving and participating in plans for fund raising and public relations and marketing.

7 The organization shall develop a written strategic plan, reviewed on a regular basis, that addresses the mission of the organization, the needs of the community, and the progress of the organization in meeting those needs.

The Advisory Committee

8 Every adult day care center shall have a body that serves as an advisory committee.

When an adult day care center is a subdivision or subunit of a multifunction organization, a committee or subcommittee of the governing body of the multifunction organization may serve as the advisory committee of the center.

For a single purpose agency, the governing body may fulfill the functions of the advisory committee if it meets the representation standard (See Standard 10, below); or, a separate advisory committee may be established.

Where there is a separate advisory committee it is recommended that the chair of that committee serve as a voting member of the governing body.

9 **The advisory committee shall meet at least twice a year and shall have an opportunity, at least annually, to review and make recommendations on program policies.**

Those policies may include:

- scope and quality of services and activities provided

- admission and discharge criteria

- service records

- quality assurance activities and findings and plan of corrective action

- program evaluation

- fees.

10 **The advisory committee shall be representative of the community and shall include family members of current or past participants and non-voting staff representatives.**

In representing a cross-section of knowledgeable community leaders, the committee may include: a nurse, possibly a community health nurse; physician; social worker; physical, occupational, recreational and/or speech therapist; lawyer; banker; local elected officials; and other community representatives who are knowledgeable about the population being served and services being provided; consumers; participants; and other interested individuals who can contribute to the strength, stability, and quality of the program.

A Written Plan of Operation

11 **The administrator shall be responsible for the development of a current, written plan of operation with approval of the governing body. The plan of operation shall be reviewed and, if necessary, revised annually.**

The plan may include:

● short- and long-range program goals

● definition of the target population, including number,
● age, and needs of participants

● geographical definition of the service area

● hours and days of operation

● description of basic services and any optional
    services

● policies and procedures for service delivery

● policies and procedures for admission and discharge

● policies and procedures for assessment and
    reassessment and the development of a plan of care
    with participants and/or family/caregiver by an
    interdisciplinary team

● staffing pattern

- a plan for utilizing community resources

- policies and procedures for recruitment, orientation, training, evaluation, and professional development of staff

- polices and procedures for recruiting, orientation, and training of volunteers

- general record policies

- statement of participant rights

- mandated reporting procedures

- marketing plan

- strategic planning

- accident, illness, and emergency procedures

- grievance procedures

- procedures for reporting suspected abuse

- payment mechanisms, funding sources, and rates

- operational budget.

A Written Emergency Plan

12 **A written plan for handling emergencies shall be developed, and posted in the center and on all center vehicles. There shall also be:**

- **staff training to ensure smooth implementation of the emergency plan and** ➤

● sufficient staff trained in CPR and first aid to assure that at least two trained staff are in the center at all times during hours of operation.

Lines of Supervision and Responsibility

13 To ensure continuity of direction and supervision, there shall be a clear division of responsibility between the governing body and the adult day care administrator.

14 An administrator shall be appointed and given full authority and responsibility to plan, staff, direct, and implement the program. The administrator shall also have the responsibility for establishing collaborative relations with other community organizations to ensure neccessary support services to participants and their families/caregivers.

15 The administrator or the individual(s) designated by the administrator shall be on site to manage the center's day-to-day operations during hours of operation. (If the administrator is responsible for more than one site, or has duties not related to adult day care administration or provision of services, the program ➤

director shall be designated for each additional site and shall report to the administrator — as stated in Part Four: Staffing)

16 An organizational chart shall be developed to illustrate the lines of authority and communication channels, and shall be provided to all staff.

Administrative Policies and Procedures

FISCAL SYSTEM

17 Every adult day care center shall demonstrate fiscal responsibility by utilizing generally accepted principles of accounting in all its financial transactions.

18 Fiscal policies, procedures, and records shall be developed to enable the administrator to meet fiscal reporting needs of the governing body and funders.

The fiscal system may:

- identify all direct and indirect costs incurred by the adult day care center

- provide for a planning process to develop annual and projected day care center budgets including specific cost allocations, year-end reconciliation, and cost reporting

- provide documentation needed for financial audits, including in-kind contributions

- provide periodic financial statements containing a balance sheet, statement of income and expenses, and changes in financial status

- allow monitoring of expenditures by identifying budget variances

- project cash flow and sources of income

- provide records of expenditures with supporting documents

- maintain billing and collection records

- provide for annual audit

- provide for timely submission of fiscal reports required by funding source(s).

FINANCIAL PLAN

19 Every adult day care center shall develop a plan to address the long-term financial needs of the program. The plan shall include projected program ➤

growth, capital purchases, projected revenue, projected expenses, and plans for fund raising.

MARKETING AND PUBLIC INFORMATION

20 Marketing and the provision of information on adult day care to the public shall be carried out.

Promotional efforts may include:

- ● brochures
- ● continuing education conferences
- ● health fairs
- ● workforce seminars
- ● open house/bazaars
- ● public service announcements, newspaper articles, TV spots, radio, advertisements
- ● signs on building and vans
- ● speaking engagements
- ● interagency networking
- ● targeted efforts to specific groups
- ● community service projects.

All centers need a marketing plan prior to start-up.

After start-up, if still necessary, it is recommended that the center develop an on-going marketing plan based on sound marketing principles.

- ● The plan may contain specific measurable objectives.

- ● Marketing funds may be addressed in the plan and included in the annual budget.

- ● The plan may be reviewed periodically to determine the degree to which objectives are met.

QUALITY ASSURANCE PLAN

21 **Every adult day care center shall develop a quality assurance plan, with specific measurable objectives, designed to meet requirements of licensing and funding sources, and professional standards.**

22 **Policies and procedures for monitoring quality of care and determining further action shall be developed by the administrator with the advice of the interdisciplinary staff team and the advisory committee (Standard 9 in this Part) and with the approval of the governing body.**

It is recommended that the quality assurance plan include provision for a Utilization Review Committee, a care plan audit, an Infection Control Committee, periodic record audits, and a measure of participant satisfaction.

The Utilization Review Committee, composed of persons not employed by the center, will benefit from similar professional training to, and communication with, center staff. Duties of the Utilization Review Committee are:

- ● to evaluate appropriateness of admissions

- ● to evaluate adequacy and coordination of provided services

- ● to evaluate continued stay, length of stay, and discharge practices

- ● to recommend in writing corrective action to the administrator.

If a Utilization Review is conducted by a funding source, those results may be substituted for a review by a Utilization Review Committee.

Care plan audits, evaluating quality of care in relation to criteria established by the interdisciplinary team, should follow these essential steps:

- ● development of outcome criteria, for presenting problems common to the center's participants

- ● description of actual outcomes, as abstracted from the center's records

- ● evaluation of actual outcomes compared with the outcome criteria, to identify problem areas

- ● documented submission of recommended corrective action to the program director

- ● reassessment of the appropriateness of the recommended corrective action, as revealed by the improved outcomes of the next audit.

An **Infection Control Committee** has responsibility for monitoring procedures implemented to guard against the spread of communicable disease and basic hygienic policies and procedures.

Periodic record audits will determine accuracy and timeliness of all data recorded.

A measure of participant satisfaction is an important element.

Personnel Policies and Practices

23 There shall be a written job description for each staff position that specifies:

● **qualifications for the job**

● **delineation of tasks**

● **lines of supervision and authority.**

24 Each employee shall receive, review, and sign a copy of the job description at the time of employment. Volunteers who function as staff also shall be provided written descriptions of responsibilities.

25 Provision shall be made for orientation of new employees and volunteers. All staff and volunteers shall receive regular in-service training and staff development that meet their individual training needs. This shall be documented.

26 Six-month probationary evaluations and annual performance evaluations, in accordance with job descriptions, shall be conducted and shall match the policy of the funding or parent organization. Staff members shall review the written evaluation, and signed copies shall be kept in locked personnel files.

27 Each employee shall receive and review a copy of the center's personnel policies at the time of employment.

In addition to the above policies and practices, it is recommended that the following be included in the written policies:

- *philosophy of the organization*
- *recruitment, hiring, evaluation, probationary, and dismissal procedures*
- *employee benefits (retirement plan, leaves, and promotion opportunities)*
- *pay practices*
- *grievance procedures.*

28 Each worker shall have an individual file containing: worker's qualifications, verification of training completed, and all performance evaluations.

29 Whenever volunteers function in the capacity of staff, all personnel policies — except financial remuneration — shall apply.

30 The program shall conform to federal and state labor laws, must be in compliance with equal opportunity guidelines, and must adhere to federal and state employment regulations.

31 Personnel files shall contain a copy of a current license or certificate, if applicable to the staff position, and certification of CPR and first aid training if applicable (with sufficient full-time staff trained so that at all times there are two trained persons in the center).

Participant Policies

32 Policies shall define the target population, admission criteria, discharge criteria, medication policy, participant rights, confidentiality, and grievance procedures.

33 No individual shall be excluded from participation in or be denied the benefits of or be otherwise subjected to discrimination in the adult day care program on the grounds of race, sex, religion, or national origin.

34 The use of chemical and/or physical restraints shall be restricted to those required in physicians' orders and shall meet provisions for their use as determined by accepted standards of practice.

35 A participant Bill of Rights shall be developed, posted, distributed to, and explained to participants, families, staff, and volunteers in the language understood by the individual.

General Record Policies

36 The adult day care center shall maintain a locked participant record system. It shall include, but is not limited to:

- ● a permanent registry of all participants with dates of admission and discharge

- ● a written policy on confidentiality and the ➤

protection of records that defines procedures governing their use and removal, and conditions for release of information contained in the records

● a written policy on conditions that require authorization in writing by the participant or the legally responsible party for release of appropriate information not otherwise authorized by law

● a written policy providing for the retention and storage of records for at least five (5) years (or in accordance with state or local requirements) from the date of the last service to the participant

● a written policy on the retention and storage of such records in the event the center discontinues operation, depending on the requirements of funding sources

● a policy and procedure manual governing the record system and procedures for all agency staff

● maintenance of records on the agency's premises in secure storage area

● notes and reports in the participant's record that are typewritten or legibly written in ink, dated,and signed by the recording person with his/her title.

PARTICIPANT RECORDS

37 The center shall maintain a record for each participant. This shall include, but is not limited to, the following:

- ● application and enrollment forms
- ● medical history and functional assessment (initial and ongoing)
- ● interdisciplinary plan of care (initial and reviews) and revisions
- ● fee determination sheet
- ● service contract
- ● signed authorizations for releases of medical information and photos, as appropriate
- ● signed authorization for participant to receive emergency medical care if necessary
- ● ancillary reports
- ● correspondence
- ● attendance and service records
- ● transportation plans
- ● results of physical examination(s)
- ● where appropriate, medical information sheet; documentation of physicians' orders; treatment, therapy, and medication notes
- ● progress notes, chronological and timely ➤

- where appropriate, discharge plan and summary
- current photograph of client
- emergency contacts.

It may be helpful to keep a daily log of services (especially therapies and treatments) provided to each participant.

ADMINISTRATIVE RECORDS

38 Administrative records shall include the following:

- personnel records (including personnel training)
- fiscal records
- statistical records
- government-related records (funding sources/ regulatory)
- contracts
- organizational records
- results of Utilization Review and care plan audit
- board meeting minutes
- advisory committee minutes
- certificates of annual fire and health inspections
- incident reports.

Community Relations

ADVOCACY

39 The center staff and board shall have a system for informing the public about long-term care, adult day care, and about the center's programs and services. Participants and/or family/caregivers shall be encouraged to advocate on behalf of adult day care and long-term care.

INFORMATION AND REFERRAL

40 Participants and their families shall be assisted in learning of and using community agencies for financial, social, recreational, educational, and medical services. (See also Part Three: Services, Standard 52).

SERVICE COORDINATION

41 The center staff shall establish linkages with other community agencies and institutions to coordinate services and form service networks.

Part Three: Services*

Recognizing that adult day care centers serve a diverse population and will have varied funding levels, and differing sources and levels of personnel and access to community resources, the National Institute on Adult Daycare recommends that the following essential services be provided. Their scope and intensity will vary with program objectives and participant need. It is necessary to recognize that, where applicable, state and local requirements will take precedence over these recommended standards.

---

*NOTE: Standards are numbered and in bold; recommendations are italicized.

The Individual Plan of Care—Essential Steps

ESSENTIAL PROGRAM COMPONENTS

42 For each individual there shall be an assessment conducted and an individual written plan of care developed, based upon services needed and available. During this process the following nine steps shall be completed, although there may be differences in the order in which they are completed by the adult day care center.

STEP ONE — INTAKE SCREENING

43 The intake screening shall be completed in order to gain an initial sense of the appropriateness of the adult day care program for the individual.

Usually conducted in a telephone call with the individual, family, or referral source, or covered on an application form, the screening includes:

- demographic information

- referral source

- living arrangement

- social history

- financial status, insurance coverage

- health/psycho-social status, diagnosis

- name(s) of primary physician and other physicians involved

- community agencies involved in providing services

- initial information on ADLs/IADLs.

44 A medical form shall be sent to the individual, the caregiver, or the physician. The form shall be completed and signed by a physician, and returned to the center, prior to admission to the program.

STEP TWO — PRE-ADMISSION ASSESSMENT

45 A pre-admission assessment shall be conducted either in the participant's home or at the center.

This includes:

- review of intake information

- review of medical forms

- ADLs/IADLs

- signing of all consents (release of information, financing, emergency information)

- signing of application.

46 As part of the assessment process, the applicant and family members or other caregivers shall ➤

> **have at least one personal interview with a program staff member.**

If a home visit by the staff was not made as part of the intake screening, then a home visit is highly recommended at this time.

STEP THREE — ENROLLMENT AGREEMENT

It is highly recommended that there be a signed enrollment agreement, including:

- *scheduled days of attendance*
- *services and goals of center*
- *unit of charges and when payable*
- *transportation agreement*
- *emergency procedures*
- *releases from liability (for example, field trips)*
- *conditions for termination from service (or discharge).*

It is preferable that the participant and/or caregiver receive a copy of the enrollment agreement and a copy of the center's grievance procedures and participant bill of rights.

STEP FOUR — INTERDISCIPLINARY TEAM ASSESSMENT

47 A comprehensive written assessment shall be completed in order to collect sufficient information to develop the individual's plan of care. The assessment shall be completed within eight (8) days of attendance in the program or within no more than 30 calendar days. The level of detail shall depend upon the level of care to be provided.

The interdisciplinary team may be composed of permanent staff, consultants, or a combination.

48 If professional services are to be provided, then each professional shall participate in the individualized assessment based on his/her professional expertise.

49 The team assessment shall identify the individual's strengths and needs, and a determination shall be made as to how the center shall serve the individual.

It is recommended that the assessment include the person's health profile (medical records, medical history, verification of medical regimen, primary physician and other specialists, and physician's restrictions), social history, formal and informal support systems, including caregiver information and assessment of caregiver stress, activities of daily living skills, mental and emotional status, community and financial resources, interests, hobbies, and past occupation.

50 A current medical report (based upon an examination completed within six months prior to admission) including diagnosis, medication, other treatment recommendations, and verification of the absence of communicable disease (including tuberculosis screening) shall be obtained from the physician prior to enrollment unless exception is necessary. Each participant shall have a physician available to contact in the event of an emergency and for ongoing care.

STEP FIVE — WRITTEN INDIVIDUAL PLAN OF CARE

51 The goal of the plan of care is to increase the functioning of the participant to the optimum level and maintain it at that level. The written plan of care shall reflect the individual's strengths, needs, and problems and shall be developed by an inter-disciplinary team through a team conference. It shall include realistic, specific, verifiable, and achievable objectives that are both long-term and short-term. Also to be identified are the services to be provided and the responsible staff.

Each individual's plan of care shall include:

● identified service needs ➤

● time-limited measurable goal(s) and objectives of
care for the participant

● services to be provided by the center and by other
sources to achieve the goal(s) and objectives.
(This will be a configuration of Essential Services
and Additional Services described later in this
section.)

The participant, family/caregiver, and other service
providers shall have the opportunity to contribute to the
development, implementation, and evaluation of the
care plan.

STEP SIX — COORDINATION OF CARE

52 The need for coordination of care shall be
considered for each participant. If coordination
of care is needed and if the person is a client of another
agency, then a care plan shall be developed in
conjunction with the services provided by that agency.

If the participant is in need of coordination of care and
is not receiving care management from another
organization or agency, then the adult day care center
could serve as care manager (provided it meets the
standards promulgated in the NICLC Care Management
Standards of 1988).*

---

* National Institute on Community-based Long-term Care. *Care Management
Standards.* Washington, D.C.: The National Council on the Aging, Inc. 1988.

STEP SEVEN — SERVICE DOCUMENTATION

53 Progress notes on each participant shall be written at least quarterly and shall reflect at least a review of the plan of care (including service needs and goals and objectives) and shall reflect the participant's status in regard to the services. Treatment notes and notes on significant events shall be recorded according to professional standards, when appropriate.

STEP EIGHT — REASSESSMENT

54 Reassessment applies to the plan of care and ongoing comprehensive functional assessments as well as the evaluation of goals and approaches that shape the plan of care. Reassessing the individual's needs and reevaluating the appropriateness of service plans shall be done when needed—but at least semi-annually.

Any significant change in the participant or family status, such as hospitalization, living arrangements, or modifications of the family support system, will prompt the need for a reassessment.

STEP NINE — DISCHARGE PLAN

Many participants take part in adult day care on a long-term basis. However, discharge plans are necessary and appropriate for those who will leave the program because of changes in need and functional status.

55 When appropriate for the participant, discharge procedures shall include:

● a discharge summary, including recommendations for continuing care

● referrals to community service agencies for appropriate services

● follow-up when appropriate.

56 Each participant and family/caregiver shall receive a minimum of two weeks' notice if the participant is to be discharged from the program. An exception to the policy shall be immediate discharge of an individual due to a sudden change in condition that makes participation a danger to self or others. The day care center shall have established written criteria for termination from the program available to participants and family/caregivers on admission.

Eight Essential Services

As more individuals with functional impairments are cared for in the community, adult day care centers are finding it necessary to respond to increased needs for professional services, needs which require more intensive care. Among these needs are varying requirements for the scope and intensity of services. If professional services are to be provided, then professional standards of provision and supervision must be maintained.

57 Each adult day care center shall make a decision on the services to be provided and take necessary and appropriate measures to assure the quality of the service.

58 These essential, core services shall be offered in all adult day care programs: Personal Care, Nursing, Social Services, Therapeutic Activities, Nutrition, Transportation, Emergency Plan, and Education. The intensity of the services shall be modified to meet the functional needs of the participants. It is anticipated that the services will be on a continuum to meet the range of client needs and with appropriate staff to supply these services. Each essential core service shall be addressed during the care planning process. The center shall provide and maintain the essential space, materials, and equipment necessary to provide these services and to protect the privacy of the participants receiving the services.

PERSONAL CARE

59 The adult day care program shall provide assistance and supervision needed with activities of daily living — walking, eating, grooming, toileting, and, when appropriate, bathing.

NURSING SERVICES

60 **Nursing Services shall be offered by all adult day care centers.**

The nurse may serve as a consultant or may be a part-time or full-time staff member. Delegation of some nursing services, such as personal care, to assistants who are trained and supervised by the nurse is part of the nursing service.

Nursing services may vary in intensity, depending on the need of the participants. Intensity is determined by both the number of participants requiring nursing services and the type of nursing service needed.

61 **According to participant needs as identified in the nursing assessment, interdisciplinary plan of care, and physician orders, the nursing service shall include a configuration of services at different levels of intensity.**

62 **All day care centers shall:**

● **assess participants' health status, including dietary needs;**

● **monitor vital signs and weight;**

● **provide health education and counseling, including nutritional advice, to participants and families;** ➤

- develop policies and procedures for personal care and train staff in their implementation;

- provide liaison with the participant's personal physician, notifying the physician (as well as the family/caregiver) of any changes in participant health status;

- coordinate the provision of other health services provided outside the center;

- train staff and supervise the use of standard protocols for communicable diseases and infection control;

- coordinate and oversee participant health records.

63 If the following services are needed by participants and if there is adequate nursing coverage, the center shall:

- administer and document medications, and observe for possible adverse reaction;

- supervise the provision of modified and therapeutic diets or supplemental feedings;

- provide observation, monitoring, and intervention for unstable medical conditions;

- provide training in self-administration of medications;

- provide restorative or rehabilitative nursing, ➤

including bladder and bowel retraining and the supervision of or provision of maintenance therapy procedures;

● provide supportive nursing such as general maintenance care of colostomy and ileostomy, change dressings, prophylactic skin care to avoid skin breakdown, foot and nail care, and routine care of incontinent participants, including incontinence supplies;

● provide emergency care;

● provide for regular inspection of drug storage conditions;

● provide any other direct nursing service requiring skilled nursing treatment.

Other nursing services that may be added are:

● intravenous, intramuscular, or subcutaneous injections;

● insertion, sterile irrigation, and replacement of catheters;

● application of dressings, involving prescription medication and aseptic techniques;

● nasogastric tube, gastrostomy, and jejunostomy feedings;

● naso-pharyngeal and tracheotomy aspirations;

● any other skilled nursing services that may be safely done in the adult day care center.

SOCIAL SERVICES

64 **Social services shall be provided by all adult day care centers.**

The social worker may serve as a consultant or may be a part-time or full-time staff member. Social services are provided to participants and their families to help them with personal, family, and adjustment problems that interfere with the effectiveness of the treatment plan. They are an essential part of care management.

According to participant needs as identified in the social assessment and interdisciplinary plan of care, social services may include a configuration of the following, depending on the level of intensity needed.

65 **All adult day care centers shall:**

● **upon enrollment, compile a social history and conduct a psychosocial assessment (mood, behavior, social patterns, life events) including formal and informal support systems, mental and emotional status, community and financial resources, and caregiver data;**

● **provide counseling to participants and families/ caregivers, assisting the participant's adaptation to the adult day care program and active involvement in the plan of care, if appropriate;**

● **arrange for other community services not provided by the adult day care center and work➤**

with these agencies to coordinate all services;

● serve as participant advocate by asserting and safeguarding the human and civil rights of the participant;

● assess for signs of mental illness and/or dementia and make appropriate referrals;

● provide discharge planning and assist in the transition and follow-up;

● provide information and referral for persons not appropriate for adult day care.

The center may:

● facilitate family conferences, serve as liaison between participant, family, and center;

● provide individual or group counseling and support to caregivers and participants;

● facilitate the development of family support groups.

THERAPEUTIC ACTIVITIES

66 The activity plan shall be integral part of the total plan of care for the individual. The planning of activities shall reflect professional understanding of the needs and abilities of the participants. Activities shall emphasize the individual participant's strengths and abilities rather than impairments and shall contribute to participant feelings of competence and accomplishment.

67 The adult day care program shall provide for a balance of purposeful activities to meet the participants' interrelated needs and interests (social, intellectual, cultural, economic, emotional, physical, and spiritual).

68 Provision shall be made for each individual to participate at his/her optimal level of functioning and to progress according to his/her own pace.

69 Activities shall be designed in a holistic manner to promote personal growth and enhance the self-image and /or to improve or maintain the functioning level of participants.

Activities offer, but are not limited to, opportunities to:

- ● maintain lifelong skills
- ● learn new skills and gain knowledge
- ● challenge and tap the potential abilities of participants
- ● participate in activities of interest
- ● improve capacity for independent functioning
- ● develop interpersonal relationships
- ● develop creative capacities

● improve physical and emotional well-being

● be exposed to and involved in activities and events within the greater community

● experience cultural enrichment

● have fun and enjoyment.

70 **Activity programming shall take into consideration individual differences in health status, lifestyle, ethnicity, religious affiliation, values, experiences, needs, interests, abilities, and skills by providing opportunities for a variety of types and levels of involvement.**

Activities may include, but are not limited to:

● individualized activities

● small and large group activities

● active and spectator participation

● intergenerational experiences

● involvement in community activities and events

● services to individuals and to the program

● outdoor activities as appropriate

● opportunities to voluntarily perform services for individuals and the program, and community groups and organizations.

71 Participants shall be encouraged to take part in activities, but may choose not to do so or may choose another activity. Reasons for non-participation shall be evaluated to determine whether it reflects personal preference or a change in activity is indicated.

72 Time shall be allowed for rest and relaxation and to attend to personal care needs.

Background noise such as conversation or music can be therapeutic, distracting, or upsetting; therefore, it is recommended that its impact on participants be carefully assessed and adjustments made as indicated.

73 Planned activities shall be available whenever the center is in operation. A monthly calendar of activities shall be prepared and posted in a visible place.

(This may be distributed to family/caregivers and others.)

74 Group daily activities shall be posted in a prominent, convenient, visible place.

It is recommended that alternative activities be planned simultaneously to allow optimum participant involvement.

75 The activities schedule shall be coordinated with other services offered at the center and with other staff.

NUTRITION AND THERAPEUTIC DIETS

76 A minimum of one meal of an adult's daily nutritional requirement as established by state and federal regulation shall be provided. Modified diets shall be provided to meet participants' needs. Snacks and fluids shall be offered as appropriate to meet the participants' nutritional needs and needs for liquids. Nutrition education and counseling shall be an integral part of the day care program.

The participant's total dietary intake is of concern but is not the center's responsibility. The center is responsible only for meals served at the center.

Special, modified, or therapeutic diets are frequently required for persons with functional impairments in an adult day care center. These terms are often used interchangeably, usually referring to a diet prescribed by a physician, which may include modifications in nutrient content, caloric value, consistency, methods of food preparation, content of specific foods, or a combination of these modifications. The most common forms of special diets are diabetic and low-salt.

77 As a minimum, an adult day care center shall supply special diabetic, low salt diets and texture modified meals when ordered by the participant's physician and included in the interdisciplinary plan of care. Food substitution may be used. Any food substitution shall be of comparable nutritional value.

78 An adult day care center shall neither admit nor continue to serve a participant whose dietary requirements cannot be accommodated by the center.

TRANSPORTATION

79 The adult day program shall provide, arrange, or contract for transportation to enable persons, including persons with handicaps, to attend the center and to participate in center sponsored outings.

The center is encouraged to use community transportation systems, where available, and/or families for the provision of transportation.

80 All program-provided and contracted transportation systems shall meet local, state, and federal regulations.

It is recommended that participants be transported no more than sixty minutes without the opportunity for a rest stop.

EMERGENCY CARE FOR PARTICIPANTS

81 A written procedure for handling emergencies shall be posted in the center. Emergency care for participants shall include:

● a written agreement with the participant or family regarding arrangements for emergency care and ambulance transportation

● written procedure for medical crises, and

● an easily located portable file on each participant, listing identifiable information (physician's name and telephone number, family's name, insurance information, current diagnosis, medications, allergies, and hospital preference) needed in emergencies. (See also Part One: Administration and Organization)

EDUCATION

82 Education shall be provided to the family/ caregivers and participants to improve the well-being and functional level of the participants and/or caregiver and shall include health teaching, nutrition, housing, range of services and benefits available, and legal and financial planning.

Education is an on-going process which is both formal and informal.

Additional Services

The following services, though not required of all centers, may be provided directly or through contractual arrangements by an adult day care center when appropriate for the center and needed by the participants: Physical, Occupational, and Speech Therapies and Medical Services. The scope and intensity of these services will vary depending upon the needs of the participants and the program of the center.

If these services are provided on an individual basis, the cost of the service is not always part of the per diem cost of adult day care. The individual or third party payor may be billed separately.

PHYSICAL THERAPY SERVICES

Physical therapy services are provided in order to restore or maintain maximum mobility, with regimens for restoration and maintenance of muscle function. Physical therapy services range from consultation regarding group exercises to individualized skilled restorative therapy.

83 **Based on the physical therapy assessment, interdisciplinary plan of care, and physician's orders, physical therapy services (which include, but are not limited to, the following) shall:**

 ● **assess participant's mobility level, strength,** ➤

range of motion, endurance, balance, gait, ability to transfer, coordination, posture, and pain level;

● provide treatment to relieve pain and/or develop, restore, or maintain functioning;

● assist participant to achieve and maintain maximum performance using physical means such as active or passive exercise, massage, heat, moist heat, ultra sound, hydrotheropy, and ice;

● establish a maintenance program and provide written and verbal instructions to center staff and the family/caregiver to assist the participant with implementation;

● recommend adaptive or assistive devices;

● train other staff to lift, move, and otherwise assist the participant;

● evaluate the home for environmental barriers and recommend changes needed for greater participant independence;

● provide skilled rehabilitation services when indicated;

● provide assistance in obtaining assistive ambulatory devices such as canes, walkers, crutches, wheelchairs, leg braces, and prosthetic devices;

● provide physical therapy procedures that include ambulation, gait training, active and passive exercise, orthotics training, prosthesis training, massage, and neuromuscular re-education.

OCCUPATIONAL THERAPY

Occupational therapy services are those services designed to increase physical status and independence in activities of daily living and to prevent further deterioration. The intensity of services provided may range from consultation for group services to individualized acute rehabilitative therapy.

84 Depending on the occupational therapy assessment, interdisciplinary plan of care, and physician orders, occupational therapy services which include, but are not limited to, the following, shall:

- administer diagnostic and prognostic tests to determine integrity of upper extremities, ability to transfer, range of motion, balance, strength and coordination, endurance, activities of daily living, and cognitive-perceptual functioning;

- teach participants adaptive techniques to overcome barriers and impediments in activities of daily living;

- teach and train other staff in the use of therapeutic, creative, and self-care activities to improve or maintain the participant's capacity for self-care and independence, and increase the range of motion, strength, and coordination;

- train the participant in the use of supportive and adaptive equipment and assistive devices;

- evaluate home for environmental barriers and recommend changes needed for greater participant independence; ➤

- provide restorative therapy when indicated, establish a maintenance program when needed to prevent deterioration, and provide written and verbal instructions to center staff and the family/ caregiver to assist the participant with implementation;

- provide occupational therapy procedures that include:
  - training or retraining in ADLs;
  - training in work simplification techniques;
  - exercises and graded activities to improve strength and range of motion;
  - sensory stimulation techniques to minimize sensory deficits;
  - coordination activities to promote increased manual dexterity;
  - evaluation and provision of needed slings or splints to increase or maintain functional use of upper extremities.

SPEECH THERAPY

Speech services are provided in order to restore impaired speech and language disorders due to stroke, laryngectomy, head trauma, and neurological diseases.

85 Speech therapy services, when indicated by the interdisciplinary team plan of care, the speech therapist's assessment, and physician orders, (which include, but are not limited to, the following) shall: ➤

● **establish a treatment program to improve communication ability and correct disorders;**

● **provide written and verbal instruction to center staff and family members in methods to assist the participant to improve and correct speech disorders;**

● **provide speech therapy procedures that include:**
  • **auditory comprehension tasks**
  • **visual and/or reading comprehension tasks**
  • **language intelligibility tasks**
  • **language expression tasks**
  • **training involving the use of alternative communication devices.**

MEDICAL SERVICES

86 **Medical services by either a staff physician or the participant's personal physician shall be provided, or arranged for, by an adult day care center that provides nursing and/or physical, speech, or occupational therapy. Physician services may be direct or indirect.**

Physician services may be direct, indirect, or a combination of both. Centers may have a physician on a part-time basis who serves as a consultant to the interdisciplinary team, and authorizes the plan of care. The physician may also serve as medical director or directly provide hands-on assessment and/or treatment. Medical services may also be provided by the participant's personal physician who participates in the development of the plan of care and is contacted when changes or emergencies occur, provides medical assessment and treatment, is informed on a regular basis of the participant's status, and retains primary responsibility for medical care. In centers where a medical director or consultant is available to act as a member of the team and authorize care, information is usually supplied to the personal physician, who may still provide the on-going medical treatment.

Optional Services

The following services are not required of all centers. They may be provided directly or through contractual arrangements by an adult day care center if appropriate for the center and needed by the participants: Dentistry; Laboratory, Radiological and Diagnostic Services; Pharmacy; Psychiatry/Psychology; Podiatry; Ophthalmology/Optometry; Audiology; and others. Services may range from consultation to prescription of assistive devices, to ongoing treatment. The scope and intensity of these services will vary depending upon the needs of the participants and the program of the center.

If these services are provided on an individual basis, the cost of the service is not always part of the per diem cost of adult day care. The individual or third party payor may be billed separately.

87 All optional services provided by the center shall meet the following general standard:

● The provider shall meet state requirements for licensure or certification.

● Space for privacy shall be provided by the center.

● Special equipment shall be available when necessary, for example, dental chair and instruments.

● If these services are provided at another location by contract with the adult day care center, the adult day care center shall be responsible for arranging or providing transportation and escort services if needed.

● The provider shall document all services rendered in the participant's medical chart. Signed and dated laboratory, radiological, and diagnostic services shall be entered in the participant's record.

Standards for these specific services, if provided, are:

DENTISTRY

88 The dentist shall:

● provide dental services, including, but not limited to, examination, oral prophylaxis, and emergency dental care to relieve pain and infection; ➤

● develop and implement written dental services and oral hygiene policies and procedures.

LABORATORY, RADIOLOGICAL, AND DIAGNOSTIC SERVICES

89 ● The adult day care center shall establish written policies to ensure that laboratory, radiological, and diagnostic services are provided as ordered by a physician.

● Findings of such services shall be reported in writing to the physician ordering the services. The center shall also keep a record of findings.

PHARMACY

90 A pharmacist shall:

● assist in the development and review of written policies and procedures regarding medication storage, distribution, recording, and disposal in the center;

● monitor at least quarterly the implementation of policies and procedures related to medication at the center;

● furnish the administrator periodically a written report on the status of medication-related services; ➤

> ● **communicate directly with participant, pharmacies, attending physician, and center staff on matters relating to an individual's drug therapy.**

A pharmacist may also contract with an adult day care center to provide a unit dose system or medisets for all participants.

PSYCHIATRIC OR PSYCHOLOGICAL SERVICES

91 The psychiatrist, psychologist, clinical social worker, or psychiatric nurse clinician shall:

● provide assessments and reassessments when indicated by the inter-disciplinary plan of care;

● act as liaison with other members of the inter-disciplinary team and with family members and referral sources that may yield information for psychiatric or psychological treatment;

● provide group counseling and techniques as indicated by a participant's need;

● provide consultation to staff regarding behavioral management, motivation strategies, and management of stressful situations such as death of a participant;

● supervision of treatment plan implementation.

Consultant services are indicated when the social worker's assessment indicates apparent mental, emotional, or behavioral problems that need further assessment/treatment.

PODIATRY

92 A podiatrist shall:

- ● provide examination, diagnosis, and treatment when indicated by the interdisciplinary plan of care;

- ● consult with adult day care center staff about foot care.

OPHTHALMOLOGY/OPTOMETRY

93 An ophthalmologist or optometrist shall provide:

- ● vision testing and eye examinations;

- ● prescription of appropriate treatment and/or vision aids;

- ● consultation with center staff regarding techniques for working with participants with visual impairments.

AUDIOLOGY

94 An audiologist shall:

● provide an audiological evaluation;

● prescribe appropriate treatment such as a hearing aid;

● consult with center staff regarding techniques for working with hearing-impaired participants.

OTHER

95 Any other services offered in the center shall meet applicable state, local, and professional requirements. Such services may include, for example, those of a cosmetologist or barber.

Part Four: Staffing*

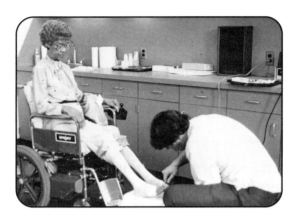

96 Staff shall be adequate in number and skills to provide the essential services described in Part Three: Services. Staff also shall be sufficient to:

● serve the number and functioning levels of adult day care participants

● meet program objectives

● provide access to other community resources.

Staff-Participant Ratio

97 There shall be at least two (2) responsible persons at the center at all times when there are   ➤

---

*NOTE: Standards are numbered and in bold; recommendations are italicized.

participants in attendance, one a paid staff member.

98 The staff-participant ratio shall be a minimum of one to six (1:6).

99 As the number and severity of participants with functional impairments increase, the staff-participant ratio shall be adjusted accordingly. Programs serving a high percentage of participants who are severly impaired shall have a staff-participant ratio of one to four (1:4).

100 Persons counted in the staff-participant ratio shall be those who spend 70 percent of time in direct service with participants.

101 If the administrator is responsible for more than one site or has duties not directly related to adult day care, a program director shall be designated for each additional site. (As also stated in Part Two: Administration and Organization.)

102 In the absence of the director, a staff member shall be designated to supervise the center.

103 To ensure adequate care and safety of participants, there shall be provision for qualified substitute staff.

104 Volunteers shall be included in the staff ratio ONLY WHEN THEY CONFORM TO THE SAME STANDARDS AND REQUIREMENTS AS PAID STAFF, meet the job qualification standards of the organization, and have designated responsibilities.

105 Each center that is co-located with another program in the same facility shall have its own staff with hours that are committed to the adult day care program.

Basic Requirements for All Staff

106 Each staff member shall be competent, ethical, and qualified for the position held.

107 References shall be checked and job histories verified for all staff and volunteers serving as staff.

108 Each employee shall have had a physical examination, including tuberculosis screening, within twelve (12) months prior to employment, and a copy of the report of the examination shall be filed in personnel records within 30 days of employment. Agency personnel policies shall also specify the intervals at which future physical examinations are required. Volunteers included in the staff ratio shall also meet this requirement. All other volunteers shall have tuberculosis screening.

109 Staff shall sign a confidentiality agreement and hold all information about participants and families in confidence, treating all participants with respect and dignity.

110 All direct service staff shall participate in each individual's plan of care, and ongoing assessment, carrying out the objectives for the participant and performing other services as required.

111 Communication. Staff members shall follow an established system for daily communication to ensure ongoing transmittal of pertinent information among staff.

112 Interdisciplinary Team. Staff responsibilities and functions shall cross staff disciplinary lines and the staff shall function as a team for the good and well being of the participants.

Staff Training and Evaluation

113 All personnel, paid and volunteer, shall be provided the following training and evaluation:

general orientation, which shall include, but not be limited to:

- purpose and goals of adult day care
- roles and responsibilities of other staff members
- behavior management techniques
- health, Universal Precautions
- information on fire and safety measures/codes
- philosophy of the program and parent organization ➤

- ● confidentiality
- ● interdisciplinary team approach
- ● participant rights
- ● needs of population served
- ● the center's policies and regulations
- ● communication skills
- ● review of basic terminology

a written probationary evaluation, which shall take place no later than at the end of the first six months of employment, signed by the employee;

a written performance evaluation, which shall occur at least annually, utilize a standardized instrument, and involve a face-to-face meeting;

opportunity for participation in in-service training sessions, (at least four (4) per year), to enhance quality of care and job performance. At the time of employment, and annually, each employee must receive training in:

- ● needs of the participants in the center's target population
- ● infection control
- ● fire, safety, and disaster plan
- ● Heimlich maneuver
- ● body mechanics/transfer techniques ➤

> ● **mandatory reporting laws of abuse/neglect**
>
> ● **CPR and first aid, as appropriate (See also Part Two: Administration and Organization)**
>
> ● **behavior management**
>
> *opportunities for additional education*, **depending on the resources of the agency.**

Staff Positions

Not every program needs a large interdisciplinary team. There are certain minimum requirements in staffing, however, that can be defined in terms of services provided. Some services cannot be delivered by those without professional training. This does not mean that all staff members must have such qualifications, but it does mean that the center must have the proper balance of professionals and paraprofessionals or non-professionals to meet adequately the needs of participants. The list in this section is intended as a guide to staff qualifications and responsibilities; it is not intended to provide detailed descriptions. Staff selection is dependent on participant needs, program design, and regulatory requirements.

It is possible to have one person responsible for multiple functions: for example, an administrator who is also responsible for nursing services or social services.

If there is only one administrative position, the functions of the Administrator and Program Director can be combined—if the applicant meets the qualifications of both positions and the person has no other adult day care duties.

Some positions may be provided as an in-kind contribution (for example, the custodian) or as a contracted service (for example, a driver provided when transportation is contracted).

Even if it has been determined that a paraprofessional can accomplish a specific task, there must be a professional person responsible for the development and supervision of services. It is necessary to consider and meet state and federal regulations for professional services.

THE CREDENTIALS SPECIFIED IN THE BRIEF DESCRIPTIONS BELOW ARE THOSE PREFERRED. PLEASE NOTE THAT THE DISCUSSION OF PROGRAM FLEXIBILITY IN THE INTRODUCTION APPLIES TO THE POSITIONS AND CREDENTIALS.

ADMINISTRATOR (may also be known as executive director).

The Administrator is responsible for the development, coordination, supervision, and fiscal control and evaluation of services provided through the adult day care program.

---

114 **The Administrator shall have a Master's degree and one year supervisory experience (full-time or equivalent) or Bachelor's degree and three years supervisory experience in a social or health service setting.**

Depending on the size and structure of the organization, some duties may be delegated to other staff. Sample duties may include the following:

● developing administrative policies and procedures

● developing resources for the center, including fund-raising, grant writing, budget development, and fiscal monitoring

● ensuring compliance with licensing and funding regulations

● facilitating and organizing advocacy efforts

● assessing the center's progress in accordance with established goals and objectives and a quality assurance plan

● implementating board policies

● hiring and supervising staff.

PROGRAM DIRECTOR (also known as center manager, site manager, center coordinator).

Under the direction of the Administrator, the Program Director organizes, implements, and coordinates the daily operation of the adult day care program in accordance with participants' needs and any mandatory requirements.

---

115 **The Program Director shall have a Bachelor's degree in health or social services or a related field, with one year supervisory experience (full-time or equivalent) in a social or health service setting.**

Sample duties may include supervision of, or direct responsibility for, the following:

● planning the day care program to meet individual needs of the participants, liaison with community agencies, and provision of services to individuals, and families when necessary

● coordinating the development and ongoing review and monitoring of each participant's individual plan of care, and making necessary program adjustments

● establishment, maintenance, and monitoring of internal management systems to facilitate scheduling and coordination of services, and for the collection of pertinent participant data

● recruitment, hiring, and general supervision of all staff, volunteers, and contractors

● training and utilization of volunteers with consideration of their individual talents and program activities to work effectively with the day care program.

SOCIAL WORKER

116 **The Social Worker shall have a Master's degree in social work and at least one year of professional work experience (full-time or the equivalent), or a Bachelor's degree in social work and two years of experience or a Bachelor's degree in another field and two years experience in a human service field.**

Depending on the setting and licensing requirements, these functions may be performed by other human service professionals, such as rehabilitation counselors, gerontologists, or mental health workers, (although they may not call themselves social workers without appropriate credentials). The duties of the social worker are included in Part Three: Services under Social Services.

NURSE

117 **The Nurse shall be a Registered Nurse (RN) with valid state credentials and a minimum of one year applicable experience (full-time or equivalent).**

It is preferable that the experience has involved working with the aging and adults who are chronically impaired and that all or part of the experience has been in a community health setting. It is also preferable that the nurse have a BSN. The duties of the nurse are included in Part Three: Services under Nursing Services.

ACTIVITIES COORDINATOR

118 **The Activities Coordinator shall have a Bachelor's degree plus one year of experience (full-time or equivalent) in social or health services or an Associate's degree in a related field plus two years of appropriate experience.**

It is preferred that the degree include a major in recreation, occupational therapy, or a related field, such as art, music, physical education, or sociology, and that experience include therapeutic recreation for older adults and those with a handicap. The duties of the Activities Coordinator are included in Part Three: Services under Therapeutic Activities.

PROGRAM ASSISTANT/AIDE

119 The Program Assistant or Aide shall have one or more years of experience in working with adults in a health care or social service setting.

Duties may include:

- provision of personal care and assistance to participants

- working with other staff members as required in implementing and carrying out services and activities and in meeting the needs of individual participants

- assisting with transportation of and escorting participants to, from, and within the center, if appropriate.

THERAPISTS

120 Physical therapists, occupational therapists, speech therapists, recreation therapists, mental health therapists, or any other therapists utilized shall have valid state credentials and one year of experience in a social or health setting.

Therapies may be provided by staff of the center or through contracts. The duties are included in Part Three: Services under Additional Services.

CONSULTANTS

121 Consultants shall be available to provide services as needed in order to supplement professional staff and enhance the program's quality.

Consulting services may be provided by contractual agreement with community groups or on an individual basis. Examples include: legal, nutrition, business and financial management, psychiatric, medical, physical therapy, occupational therapy, speech therapy, pharmacy, and therapeutic recreation.

SECRETARY/BOOKKEEPER

122 The Secretary/Bookkeeper shall have at least a high school diploma or equivalent and skills and training to carry out the duties of the position.

Duties may include:

● assisting in development and maintenance of a recordkeeping system for the program

● performing tasks necessary to handle correspondence and office activities

- answering the telephone in a courteous and informative manner

- bookkeeping, maintaining of financial records, and billing for services.

DRIVER

123 **The Driver shall have a valid and appropriate state driver's license, a safe driving record, and training in first aid and CPR (cardiopulmonary resuscitation). The driver shall meet any state requirements for licensure or certification.**

The driver, who could also be a program aide in the center, should be aware of basic transfer techniques and safe ambulation. Experience in working with adults who are impaired is desirable, as is the successful completion of a defensive driving course, training in sensitivity to the aging, and, where appropriate, passenger assistance training. Sample duties may include:

- provide round trip transportation from patient home to center, and provide escort service as needed to ensure participant safety

- ensure that all appropriate safety measures are carried out while transporting participants

- report behavioral changes or unusual incidents of participants to appropriate professional staff and consult with other program staff as necessary.

VOLUNTEERS

124 The Volunteers shall be individuals or groups who desire to work with adult day care participants and shall take part in program orientation and training. The duties of volunteers shall be mutually determined by volunteers and staff. Duties, to be performed under the supervision of a staff member, shall either supplement staff in established activities or provide additional services for which the volunteer has special talents.

Sample duties may include:

● working under the direction of paid program and professional staff, carrying out program activities

● providing supplemental activities (such as parties and special events)

● fund-raising and assisting in public relations

● leading activities in areas of special knowledge, experience, or expertise.

Part Five: Facility*

The physical environment of the adult day care center has great potential as a therapeutic tool. A well-planned environment has the appropriate supports and cues to enhance the participants' ability to function as independently as possible and to engage in program activities. The environment plays an even more significant role as an individual's level of impairment increases. There is no "best design" or "perfect environment," but creativity and imagination are two key factors largely responsible for an effective environmental design.

In designing an adult day care center, planners must create an environment sensitive and supportive to the principles of adult day care that will:

---

*NOTE: Standards are numbered and in bold; recommendations are italicized.

● maximize the functional level of the participant and encourage independence to the greatest degree possible;

● build on the participants' residual strengths, while recognizing their limitations and impairments;

● establish for the participant a sense of control and self-determination, regardless of his/her level of functioning;

● assist in maintaining the physical and emotional health of the participant while preventing further debilitation whenever possible.

Location

125 **Selection of a site for a center shall be based on information about potential participants in its service area and be made in consultation with other agencies, organizations, and institutions serving older individuals and those with functional impairements, as well as considering the availability of a suitable site.**

Factors to consider in selecting a site include:

● demographic information and projections about potential participants and caregivers in the service area

● projections of actual use

● input from, and consultations with, other agencies and institutions in regard to community needs

AN ADULT DAY CARE CENTER

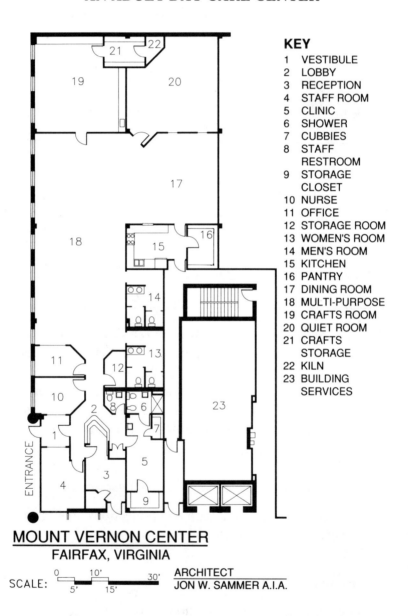

KEY

1 VESTIBULE
2 LOBBY
3 RECEPTION
4 STAFF ROOM
5 CLINIC
6 SHOWER
7 CUBBIES
8 STAFF
   RESTROOM
9 STORAGE
   CLOSET
10 NURSE
11 OFFICE
12 STORAGE ROOM
13 WOMEN'S ROOM
14 MEN'S ROOM
15 KITCHEN
16 PANTRY
17 DINING ROOM
18 MULTI-PURPOSE
19 CRAFTS ROOM
20 QUIET ROOM
21 CRAFTS
   STORAGE
22 KILN
23 BUILDING
   SERVICES

ENTRANCE

MOUNT VERNON CENTER
FAIRFAX, VIRGINIA

SCALE: 0   10'   30'
        5'   15'

ARCHITECT
JON W. SAMMER A.I.A.

AN ADULT DAY CARE CENTER
IN A SENIOR CENTER

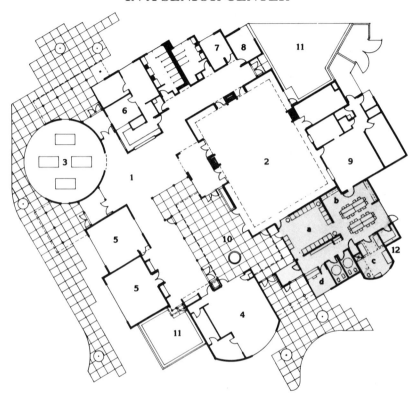

LOS VOLCANES SENIOR CENTER
ALBUQUERQUE, NEW MEXICO

40'/12m

ARCHITECTS
MAHLMAN & MILES

KEY

1	LOBBY/LOUNGE	9	KITCHEN
2	SOCIAL HALL	10	COURTYARD
3	BILLIARDS	11	GRASS
4	ARTS/CRAFTS	**12**	**ADULT DAY CARE**
5	CLASS		**a LOUNGE**
6	OFFICE		**b DINING/ARTS & CRAFTS**
7	MEDICAL		**c MEDICAL MODULE**
8	LOUNGE		**d OFFICE**

- accessibility to the greatest number of people

- proximity to, and number of, other adult day care centers in the community serving the same population, in order to avoid the duplication of services

- proximity to other services and facilities, such as therapies and medical care

- convenience to public or private transportation

- safety and security of participants and staff.

Space

126 **The facility shall comply with applicable state and local building regulations, and zoning, fire, and health codes or ordinances.**

127 **When possible, the facility shall be located on the street level. If the center is not located at street level, it is essential to have a ramp and/or elevators. An evacuation plan for relocation of participants shall also be in place in the event of a power outage.**

128 Each adult day care center, when it is co-located in a facility housing other services, shall have its own separate identifiable space for main activity areas during operational hours. Certain space can be shared, such as the kitchen and therapy rooms.

129 The facility shall have sufficient space to accommodate the full range of program activities and services.

130 The facility shall provide at least sixty (60) square feet of program space for multi-purpose use for each day care participant.

It is strongly recommended that centers serving a significant number of people with cognitive impairment or who use adaptive equipment for ambulation or medical equipment provide eighty to one hundred (80 - 100) square feet per participant.

Note: In determining adequate square footage, only those activity areas commonly used by participants are to be included. Dining and kitchen areas are to be included only if these areas are used by participants for activities other than meals. Reception areas, storage areas, offices, restrooms, passage ways, treatment rooms, service areas, or specialized spaces used only for therapies are not to be included when calculating square footage.

131 The facility shall be flexible and adaptable to accommodate variations of activities (group and/or individual) and services.

132 The center shall provide and maintain essential space necessary to provide services and to protect the privacy of the participants receiving the services. (See Part Three: Services)

The stress of providing adult day care is high, and environmental supports are essential to assist staff members to maintain good staff morale and job satisfaction.

133 There shall be sufficient private space to permit staff to work effectively and without interruption.

In addition, it is highly recommended that staff have a separate restroom and separate eating place.

The emotional strain of caregiving is also tremendous for families and other caregivers.

134 There shall be an identified separate space available for caregivers to have private discussions with staff.

135 There shall be adequate storage space for program and operating supplies.

136 The center's restrooms shall be located as near the activity area as possible, preferably no more than forty (40) feet away. The facility shall include at least one toilet for each ten (10) participants. Programs that have a large number of participants that require more scheduled toileting or assistance with toileting shall have at least one toilet for each eight participants. The toilets shall be equipped for use by mobility-limited persons, easily accessible from all program areas, and one or two of the toilet areas should be designed to allow assistance from one or two staff.

If there is a medical clinic/health treatment room in the facility, it is highly recommended that there also be an adjacent bathroom with a shower accessible to those with a handicap.

Some participants may have difficulties with incontinence. Arrangements can be made with the family to leave an extra set of clothing at the center. If laundry services are available on site, and if staff time is available, they may be utilized.

137 In addition to space for program activities, the facility shall have a rest area and designated ➤

areas to permit privacy and to isolate participants who become ill or disruptive, or may require rest. It shall be located away from activities areas and near a restroom and the nurse's office.

138 A lighted parking area with sufficient space for getting on and off vehicles shall be available for the safe arrival and departure of participants .

It is recommended that there be sufficient parking available to accommodate family caregivers, visitors, and staff. It is also recommended that a minimum of two parking spaces be identified as parking for those with a handicap and that these spaces be at least l3 feet wide and located near the entrance door.

It is recommended that outside space accessible to indoor areas be available for outdoor activities and accessible to those with a handicap. These could include smooth walkways, seating for resting or watching activities, recreational space, and a garden area. The area should have a fence or landscaping to create a boundary in order to prevent participants from wandering, and it should be easily supervised by staff. Outside furniture should be sturdy and safely arranged.

Atmosphere and Design

139 The design shall facilitate the participants' movement throughout the center and encourage involvement in activities and services. The environment shall reinforce orientation and awareness of the surroundings by providing cues and information about specific rooms, locations, and functions that help the participant to get his/her orientation to time and space.

It is recommended that some of these cues be the extensive use of signs and the color coding of specific areas of the facility.

140 A facility shall be architecturally designed in conformance with the requirements of Section 504 of the Rehabilitation Act of 1973 to accommodate individuals with a handicap and meet any state and local barrier-free requirements.

ANSI Standard A117.1-1980, "Specification for Making Buildings and Facilities Accessible to and Usable by Physically Handicapped People," is recommended as an excellent guide.

The atmosphere must be warm and inviting. It is desirable to avoid an institutional appearance and to offer an atmosphere which provides an opportunity for social contacts, both casual and structured, but also allows for individuals who prefer being alone from time to time.

141 Illumination levels in all areas shall be adequate, and careful attention shall be given to avoiding glare. Attention shall be paid to lighting in transitional areas such as outside to inside and different areas of the center.

142 Sound transmission shall be controlled. Excessive noise, such as fan noise, shall be avoided.

Recommended methods of sound control may include acoustical ceiling surfaces, sound deadening carpeting, fabric hangings, partitions between activity areas, and separation of noisy rooms such as the kitchen.

Amplification devices such as assistive listening devices, public address (PA) systems, and audio loops for those with hearing impairment are recommended for consideration.

Older adults with disabilities are prone to hypo- or hyperthermia requiring temperature adjustments to their specific needs.

143 Comfortable conditions shall be maintained within a comfortable temperature range. Excessive drafts shall be avoided uniformly throughout the center.

144 Sufficient furniture shall be available for the entire participant population present. Furnishings shall accommodate the needs of participants and be attractive, comfortable, and homelike, while being sturdy and safe.

Considerations for selecting furniture may include washability, safety, and the use of arrangements which encourage independence and, perhaps, small group interaction. Recliners are suggested for participants' needs and can also be used as a therapeutic tool for rest and/or enhancing circulation and breathing.

145 Straight-backed chairs with arms shall be used during activities and meals.

According to the needs of participants and the level of care provided (for example, for skin or wound care), it is recommended that beds, cots, or sofabeds may be available in a designated area.

146 An adult day care facility shall be visible and recognizable as a part of the community.

Outside signs can be useful to attract participants and to educate the community.

147 **The entrance to the center shall be clearly identified.**

Directional signs may also be needed if the entrance to the center is not at the front of the building.

It is recommended that signs be visible from the road, attractive and appropriate for a service for adults, and have large lettering.

148 **The entrance to the facility shall be appealing and protective to participants and others.**

It is recommended that the entrance be well lighted, accessible to individuals with handicaps, and a short distance from the point of arrival.

Also recommended is a covering over the outside entrance to protect participants from inclement weather. The ideal entrance would have a canopy to allow people to drive under to discharge participants.

149 **When necessary, arrangements shall be made with local authorities to provide safety zones for those arriving by motor vehicle and adequate traffic signals for people entering and exiting the facility.**

150 Internal signs shall be used to facilitate participants' ability to move about the center independently and safely.

151 A telephone shall be available for participant use.

Safety and Sanitation

152 The facility and grounds shall be safe, clean, and accessible to all participants.

153 The facility shall be designed, constructed, and maintained in compliance with all applicable local, state, and federal health and safety regulations.

154 There shall be an area for labeled medications, secured and stored apart from participant activity areas. If medications need to be refrigerated, they should be in a locked box —if not in their own refrigerator.

155 Safe and sanitary handling, storing, preparation, and serving of food shall be assured. If meals are prepared on the premises, kitchen applicances and equipment must meet state and local requirements.

156 Toxic substances, whether for activities or cleaning, shall be stored in an area not accessible to participants.

157 At least two well-identified exits shall be available. Nonslip surfaces or bacteria-resistant carpets shall be provided on stairs, ramps, and interior floors.

158 Alarm/warning systems are necessary to insure the safety of the participants in the center in order to alert staff to potentially dangerous situations. Call bells shall be installed or placed in the rest areas, restroom stalls, and showers.

159 Universal Precautions shall be used by all staff.

160 An evacuation plan shall be posted in each room.

161 The facility shall be free of hazards, such as high steps, steep grades, and exposed electrical cords. Steps and curbs shall be painted and the edges of stairs marked appropriately to highlight them.

162 All stairs, ramps, and bathrooms accessible to those with handicaps shall be equipped with properly anchored handrails.

Handrails throughout the center may be needed if the functional level of the participants requires such assistance.

It is recommended that an alarm system be used for participants who wander. It is also recommended that an alarm/warning system be installed at exit ways not regularly used by participants.

163 Procedures for fire safety as approved by the local fire authority shall be adopted and posted, including provisions for fire drills, inspection and maintenance of fire extinguishers, periodic inspection, and training by fire department personnel. The center shall conduct and document quarterly fire ➤

drills and keep reports of drills on file. Improvements shall be made based on the fire drill evaluation. Smoke detectors shall also be used.

Sprinkler systems are highly recommended.

164 Emergency first-aid kits shall be visible and accessible to staff. Contents of the kits shall be replenished after use and reviewed as needed. Personnel trained in first aid and CPR shall be on hand whenever participants are present. Infection control procedures, as delineated in Center for Disease Control standards, shall be followed by all staff. All staff shall be trained in and use Universal Precautions.

165 There shall be sufficient maintenance and housekeeping personnel to assure that the facility is clean, sanitary, and safe at all times.

166 Maintenance and housekeeping shall be carried out on a regular schedule and in conformity with generally accepted sanitation standards, without interfering with the program.

167 Although it is important to assure that insect infestation is controlled, staff must be aware of the respiratory problems of participants when insecticide is used. Its use shall be scheduled at a time when participants are not in the center.

168 A sufficient budget shall be provided for equipment maintenance, repair, or replacement.

169 If smoking is permitted, an adequately ventilated special area away from the main program area shall be provided and supervised.

Part Six: Evaluation*

Evaluations provide information concerning the effectiveness in reaching established goals and objectives. Evaluation is a process whereby information is secured by the agency for the purpose of making appropriate program and/or structural changes. Evaluations include an analysis of data collected and a comparison of the planned expectations and actual achievements, based on prevailing community standards of care.

The administrator of the adult day care program is responsible for seeing that the program evaluation is done on a regular basis and reported to the governing body. The governing body must ensure that evaluations result in positive and constructive actions for improving agency effectiveness.

---

*NOTE: Standards are numbered and in bold; recommendations are italicized.

The program evaluation may be conducted either internally or externally—if conducted internally, it is recommended that it include individuals not directly affiliated with the center. If conducted externally, it is recommended that composition of the interdisciplinary team include persons with expertise concerning specialized populations being served.

The NIAD self-assessment instrument is recommended as the guide for this evaluation.

170 **The evaluation process selected by the agency shall examine the adult day care program on three levels: the participant/caregiver/staff level, the agency-program level, and the community level. The evaluation shall include resources invested, the productivity of performance, and the resulting benefits.**

171 **Each adult day care program shall have a written plan for the evaluation of its operation and services. The program's goals and objectives shall be reviewed at least annually but not all evaluation components need to be done that often. The plan shall include:**

- **the purpose and reason for the evaluation**

- **the timetable for initiating and completing the evaluation**

- **the parties to be involved**   ➤

- the areas that will be addressed

- the methods to be used in conducting the evaluation

- how the information will be used once it is completed, and

- with whom the information will be shared.

172 Funding to cover the costs of program evaluation shall be included in the program budget.

173 Program evaluation shall focus on both quality assurance and operational components. These are the measurable indicators that shall be reviewed.

Quality Assurance Indicators

174 There shall be a quality assurance component that routinely assesses and measures the impact of the program on the participants, caregivers, and the community to determine that the program is meeting their needs. This shall include:

- participant and/or family satisfaction with ➤

service and evaluation as part of an exit survey;

● data collected from the grievance procedure;

● community surveys; and/or

● ongoing care plan review and evaluation and random review of records by the interdiciplinary team;

● an objective participant assessment tool that measures social, health, functional, and cognitive status at intake and at regular intervals thereafter.

This tool can be used to measure both individual and group outcomes, to identify the program's strengths and weaknesses, and to provide some guidance for program improvement.

175 A written report of the quality assurance measures, plans of action and/or correction shall be made at regular intervals and shared with the governing body.

Operational Component Measures

176 Fiscal — The fiscal system and fiscal plan shall be evaluated in comparison to the standards in this document and to those of the governing body.

177 Facility — The facility shall be evaluated in comparison to the standards in this document and a plan developed to address needs regarding location and space, atmosphere and design, safety and sanitation, and comfort.

178 Records and data — Each organization shall establish a record-keeping system that meets the external state licensing/certification/funding requirements, on-going internal management needs of the organization, meets internal program goals for client services, and supports service delivery. Each record-keeping system shall be evaluated according to the standards in this document and to those of the governing body.

179 Services — Services provided shall be evaluated in comparison to the standards in this document with particular emphasis on the level and intensity of services in relation to participant needs.

180 Personnel — Personnel policies and records shall be evaluated according to the standards in this document and to those of the governing body.

181 Marketing objectives and the tools and techniques used in marketing shall be evaluated as a component part of strategic planning. Marketing should be evaluated in relation to community image (including potential referral sources and consumer groups), and the census of the program (the number of people served and the target population).

182 Administration — The authority structure, including Board of Directors, administration, and federal/state/local government, shall be evaluated in terms of its relationship to the goals of the organization.

It is recommended that the areas addressed include:

● *a mission statement that directs policy*

● *organizational structure*

● *decision-making authority*

● *relationship of governing body to operations and the advisory committee.*

Guidelines for Adult Day Care Centers Serving Individuals with Alzheimer's Disease and Other Dementias

Preface

As a significant part of the standards development project undertaken by the National Council on the Aging/ National Institute on Adult Daycare (NCOA/NIAD), the special considerations necessary in serving participants with dementia must be highlighted. This section relates those considerations to the overall standards in the preceding section. This section reiterates points included in the standards which are to be emphasized in serving individuals with dementia. It also modifies and adds to other requirements proposed in the standards.

Note

The abbreviation AD for Alzheimer's Disease is used throughout these guidelines in referring to persons diagnosed with Alzheimer's Disease or other dementias which cause memory loss and a decline in intellectual functioning.

Philosophy

The uniqueness of the needs of persons with AD has led adult day care centers to adapt their programs to serve this growing population. Because AD causes physical changes to the brain that affect every area of behavior and functioning, serving persons with AD in an adult day care center requires developing a very different approach to the care provided traditionally.

A successful adult day care program for persons with AD is characterized by:

■ staff trained in the appropriate ways of communicating and responding to participants who have lost the ability to think, act, and convey needs in conventional ways

(Using traditional methods of communicating can place participants in threatening situations, which may lead to behaviors that have been labeled as "problems." To prevent these situations, staff members must be trained to convey acceptance of the participant's behavior in both their verbal and non-verbal communication and develop alternative strategies to resolve problems and conflicts.)

■ a commitment to make a safe and supportive environment for the participant with AD

(Creating this environment requires understanding the disease process and making adaptations to compensate for participants' losses.)

■ a structured program of non-threatening activities that promotes the participants' dignity and self-esteem and maintains their cognitive, physical, and psychosocial functioning at the highest possible level for as long as possible

■ educational and supportive services to family/caregivers, designed to strengthen their caregiving abilities and coping skills.

Symptoms of Alzheimer's Disease

Alzheimer's Disease is a progressive degenerative disease that causes pathological changes in the brain. The symptoms include gradual memory loss, decline in the ability to perform routine tasks, impairment of judgment, disorientation, behavior changes, difficulty in learning, and loss of communication skills. Behavior changes most frequently experienced include suspiciousness, insecurity and anxiety, pacing, fidgeting, and, for some persons, aggressiveness and wandering.

Although persons with AD lose their abilities at various rates and to different degrees, all are placed at a considerable disadvantage and risk because of these losses. Because there are no obvious, visible physical characteristics of the disease, relating to these "invisible" losses is one of the more difficult aspects of caring for persons with AD.

The adult day care center must be prepared to deal with the unique characteristics of AD. The most common symptoms of AD which must be confronted in an adult day care center follow.

● **The loss of the ability to reason and make decisions.** As far as possible, staff must manage behavior by accepting it. Arguing, confronting, and convincing are counterproductive in dealing with persons with AD. Distracting the person from a troublesome behavior is often successful.

● **Shortened attention span.** Concentrating long

enough to complete an activity becomes increasingly difficult for the person with AD as the disease progresses. Activities must be analyzed and structured to accommodate each person's needs. Participation in traditional groups may become difficult.

● **Disorientation and memory loss.** A participant with AD cannot process a lot of details at once or may not be able to remember well-learned information. For example, participants may be unable to recall the location of certain rooms in the center or be incapable of following simple directions.

● **Slowed reaction time.** Response to instructions is often delayed. Even if the participant may understand an instruction, he or she will take a longer time to react in an appropriate manner. The individual may also need active encouragement to initiate or follow through on an activity.

● **Wandering behavior.** Some persons with AD may wander. The reasons for this symptom are unclear, but wandering may result from being overstimulated, anxious, or uncomfortable. Aimless wandering may be a way of expressing that the person feels lost, bored, restless, or in need of exercise. The person may be searching for something or some place previously known. But, for whatever reason it occurs, wandering behavior is a safety risk for adult day care centers unless the environment is modified to monitor exits from the building — while physically structured to allow for safe wandering.

● **Perceptual problems.** The ability to interpret information from the eyes, ears, and other sensory organs is affected with AD. The participant may become lost in the center, may be unable to recognize common objects or familiar persons, or have difficulty perceiving spatial relationships.

● **Needs for assistance.** There will be an increased need for assistance in the instrumental activities of daily living (IADLs) and in the activities of daily living (ADLs). Needs for feeding and toileting assistance, for example, can be of special importance in planning to serve participants with AD in an adult day care center.

The progression of Alzheimer's disease and stages of its progress have been described in simple and complex ways. Most significant is the recognition that both cognitive and functional impairments will increase although for each individual the disease will progress differently. It is necessary to anticipate the progress of the illness, to the extent possible, and its effect upon the center in order to plan effectively.

Introduction

These guidelines are not intended for use only by those centers that exclusively serve participants with dementia, nor is it being recommended that those participants always be served in separate, segregated programs or centers. Rather, these are recommendations for the use of the many adult day care centers throughout the country that are now serving some participants with AD. It should be noted that, if recommendations appear to be contradictory to the center's operating policies, it may be necessary for the center director or governing body to reconsider the target population it intends to serve and is able to serve. Because of the special needs of individuals with AD, a conscious, informed decision on the part of the governing body and director on how best to serve them is essential. A decision on integrated versus segregated programming is also essential. If an integrated program is chosen (or if it is the only option, as is often the case), then the welfare of the entire group of participants must be examined. As the composition of the group changes, it will be necessary to re-examine regularly the effects of the integrated program.

All individuals, groups, and centers are, of course, different. However, there are some commonly agreed upon principles of good care that form the foundation of these recommended guidelines. For example, experienced providers emphasize:

● the importance of routine for the participant with AD and the value of repeatedly following a regular daily schedule;

● sufficient flexibility to provide alternatives that accommodate unanticipated needs and events;

● communication — compensating for the diminished communication skills of participants and using words and non-verbal actions to encourage desirable or necessary behavior;

● behavior acceptance (rather than behavior modification) — while taking measures to avoid triggering "problem" behaviors;

● a sensitivity to timing and deliberate and conscious

avoidance of hurrying the participants; and

● the ability of the staff to recognize the verbal and non-verbal cues of participants.

Three factors in adult day care programs take on added importance when serving participants with AD: **(1)** the role of the family and/or caregiver, **(2)** the use of adult day care to offer respite, and **(3)** the staff.

(1) The family/caregiver, in these programs, as well as the participant is a client of the center. These guidelines address the many points at which the family/caregiver must be involved. Family members other than the primary caregiver may also need to be involved in service and placement decisions and processes.

(2) Respite, or relief, is one of the benefits of adult day care. The program not only provides essential relief to the family/caregiver; it also offers respite to the participant— that is, a change from the home environment—and the expectations and emotions of the family/caregiver—and an opportunity to interact with others.

(3) Because of the special needs and unique behaviors of participants with AD, it is important that staff possess certain personality traits and attitudes. Many of these qualities, such as commitment, empathy, patience, flexibility, and a sense of humor, are common to staff in all adult day care programs. Staff must always possess energy and enthusiasm for their work but in this type of program they also need to project a feeling of calmness in their approach. As in other adult day care centers, staff must be interested in and concerned for the participants and sensitive to their special needs. They should have a desire to help people and engage them in meaningful activities that are fun and creative, yet age appropriate. They must also respect the person for whom he/she is and accept the individual's strengths and abilities without unrealistic expectations for improvement.

The qualifications required by the center should be flexible enough to consider the applications of individuals who are open to learning and have a genuine interest in working with this special population. It is often more difficult to re-train someone who has learned an approach that is inappropriate for the program than it is to take someone with no experience and train him/her.

Staff who remain in this field generally possess perseverance and optimism. They derive their greatest satisfaction not from the progress they see but the happiness and enjoyment found in the day care experience and the positive impact they have on the participants' and family/caregivers' quality of life.

The Guidelines

Administration and Organization

In addition to the requirements for Administration and Organization in the overall standards, the adult day care center serving participants with AD should:

- ● assure the representation of family members (of current and/or past participants) in the governing body and/or advisory committee;

- ● develop an overall plan which allows a staffing pattern that responds to changes in the mix of the participant population;

● adopt clearly defined admission and discharge criteria, in writing on admission, based upon the center's ability to manage participants and provide safe care in a group setting — and provide those criteria to the family/caregiver (addressing, for example, participants who become: assaultive, with threatening behavior; non-ambulatory; unable to be contained; in need of the continuous attention of a staff member; or do not otherwise benefit from the program);

● allow for an orientation period to maximize adjustment — and allow for additional staff attention during this period;

● adopt organizational policies that recognize and provide a deliberate response to the unique behaviors of the participants (for example, a policy on wandering); and

● develop a plan for community education, working with local community resources such as the Area Agency on Aging and Alzheimer's Association chapter — in order to encourage families to begin using adult day care earlier in the disease process.

Services

Individual plan of care

The development of the individual plan of care should proceed as indicated in the overall standards with some additional provisions. There is an added emphasis on information gathered prior to admission and the role of the caregiver in communication — the latter necessitated by the diminished communication skills of the participants. There is value in including in the pre-admission process a visit to the home to assess the environment and family interaction. The home visit may also result in observations and recommendations related to the home environment of help to the family/caregiver. Also, during intake special attention must be paid to assessing functional ability and the evaluation of behavior.

The development of the plan of care should include:

● the involvement of the family/caregiver in all phases of the plan of care from admission to discharge;

● a diagnosis, by a physician, of probable Alzheimer's disease or other dementias;

● an assessment that includes the participant's physical, cognitive, behavioral, social/emotional, and mental status as well as input from the family/caregiver that contributes information on the participant's history, former occupations, interests, routine activities, hobbies, and former coping mechanisms;

● the encouragement of a thorough medical, mental health, and mental status assessment for dementia to rule out depression or other treatable causes for apparent dementia;

● assessment of social supports (including services available) for the participant and the family/caregiver and an evaluation of caregiver status;

● a service plan that includes and emphasizes short-term as well as long-term goals, with identifiable objectives, and that relates to the care plan;

- provision for a review of the plan of care at least every three months, or more often, if necessary;

- ongoing family conferences, education, and counseling, including the encouragement of an assessment (above);

- ongoing monitoring of mental health status to watch especially for signs of depression; and

- in planning for discharge from the program, working with the family/caregiver to identify options, facilitate the transition, and assist in making new arrangements for care.

Essential and Additional Services

All of the Essential Services described in the overall standards are necessary; the Education Services, especially those offered to the family/caregiver, should be a strong component. Also, an added function for the Nursing Service is that of working with the Social Worker to serve as liaison with the family caregiver.

Essential Services should also include access and referral to other respite services, appropriate medical services, in-home services, and development or maintenance of support groups for caregivers (including psychotherapy groups, if necessary).

Therapeutic Activities

Although a component of Essential Services in the standards, Therapeutic Activities should be emphasized and focused on for these programs. In all cases, the therapeutic activity plan must be an integral part of the overall plan of care.

The major goal of the Therapeutic Activity program is to develop structured, non-threatening activities that preserve the participants' dignity and maximize their remaining abilities and assets. This includes reinforcing the ADLs of which they continue to be capable. Therapeutic Activities are part of the structure of the entire day, a daily schedule that has a regular plan and pattern and stresses routine and regularity because participants generally find comfort in predictability and consistency.

Preferred characteristics of activities include: the use of small groups (with a staff trained in group process skills); a definite pattern to the daily schedule of activities, coupled with the ability of a staff to adapt activities to meet unpredictable participant changes; and the possibility of individual programming, if necessary. Also recommended is the use of partialization (breaking down activities into a series of steps in order to accommodate a shortened period of concentration and to increase the likelihood of successful completion, rather than frustration and increased stress, as the outcome).

In addition to the overall standards for Therapeutic Activities, there should be a comprehensive program of activities that:

- provides enjoyable pleasurable experiences

- provides a positive outlet for energy and emotions

- provides creative opportunities for self expression

- structures time

- provides relaxation and stress-release

- accommodates wandering and produces a safe climate

- helps to increase feelings of self-worth

● provides physical fitness activities

● provides continued contact with the community, including field trips, when appropriate

● provides opportunities for peer relationships and

● is designed to maintain participants' maximum level of functioning.

The Therapeutic Activities program should also provide:

● individual plans, based upon the leisure interest history and assessment, with monitoring of progress

● activity flow patterns that include both deliberately quieting and more stimulating activities at the most appropriate times of the day
      (For example, more demanding and structured activities are often more successful in the morning. Since anxiety and agitation usually increase as the end of the day approaches, creative expressive therapies such as music may be more appropriate then.)

● opportunities for walking in a safe environment

● separation of higher/lower level functioning groups or planning of parallel activities to adjust to the abilities of the group, when appropriate

● activities that are age-appropriate, enhance self-esteem, and stimulate long-term memory

● attention to quality and quantity of sensory stimuli, with the appropriate level of sensory stimulation provided without unnecessarily contributing toward participants' anxiety
      (Participants are likely to have a limited capacity

to process large amounts of stimulation and sort out pertinent stimuli from background.)

● the opportunity for participants to identify tasks that can be done and sufficient support to ensure success in order to regain a sense of control (with the use of techniques such as partialization, for example).

NOTE: The references listed in the Resources section include materials that describe actual activities, with schedules, materials, and rationale.

Staffing

It is essential that staff members have knowledge of dementias and concomitant communication (verbal and nonverbal) skills, behavior management skills, and group process skills, as well as the awareness of specific losses likely to be experienced — especially the loss of reasoning. It is necessary for the staff to anticipate, to prevent (when possible), and to prepare to handle the most likely situations, including, for example, difficulty in group participation, high anxiety, aggressive behavior, wandering, and incontinence.

The interdisciplinary team approach described in the overall standards is especially important in programs serving these participants because of the need for a team approach to program planning and problem solving.

In addition to the Staffing Requirements stated in the overall standards, the adult day care center should:

● consider its staffing needs in terms of job functions, the numbers of staff to be determined by the numbers of participants, and levels of disability;

● maintain a higher staff-to-participant ratio (1:4 or higher, especially with a population with a high level of impairment);

● assure the presence of at least two (2) staff members at all times;
  (The presence of at least three (3) staff members is recommended when more than one or two participants may be present.)

● provide additional staff orientation, in-service training, and staff development, especially on AD, the family/caregiver and family functioning, communication with participants with AD, and group process skills;

● provide additional staff support to increase staff satisfaction, including respite for staff, rotation of assignments, active cross-disciplinary cooperation, and the sharing of unpleasant tasks;

● provide regularly scheduled staff support groups and recognition of accomplishments;

● provide training in preventing and handling aggression and other difficult behaviors;

● consider the special issues in the use of volunteers, and provide maximum consistency and training, if they are used.

Facility

The physical facility and operation should both protect the participant from injury and maintain his or her rights at the same time. As the participant's level of impairment increases, the environment takes on even greater significance. Because participants with dementia have problems with linking the past and present, the environment should facilitate that linkage by making the environment as non-institutional and as comfortable (for both participants and staff) as possible.

In addition to the Facility requirements of the overall standards, the facility should:

- offer greater square footage of common activity space per participant than the overall standards require (preferably 80-100 square feet per participant);

- be self-contained, if possible, with at least a minimum number of passageways, corridors, and exit doors;

- provide reduced sensory stimulation (for example, limiting noise, traffic, reflective surfaces—such as mirrors and very shiny floors—and wall and floor coverings with complex patterns);

- make careful use of safety precautions (name tags and alarm systems, for example);

- be free of ambiguities and obstacles because of participants' diminished capacity to perceive the environment;

- employ the use of cues (for example, circular clocks, calendars, and signs) so that physical factors will enhance and support functioning, rather than add to confusion;

- use locks in accordance with local fire and safety requirements;

- ● use no physical restraints;

- ● use modifications, such as disguised doors, (also in accordance with local fire and safety requirements) to control wandering, since an obvious open door may invite leaving;

- ● test out modifications to the environment (more than once, if necessary) before fully implementing them to be certain that the response to the change is a positive one;

- ● offer a space for personal belongings (including a change of clothing);

- ● provide at least one toilet for each six participants plus more than one toilet stall large enough to permit assistance from one or two staff members;

- ● provide a hand-held shower or shower area for participants who are incontinent;

- ● make special arrangements for fire drills with a plan for staff supervision of participants so that the evacuation process takes place without undue distress and anxiety;

- ● limit access to the telephone (and provide supervision for its use) to participants who would benefit from its use;

- ● store all materials (crafts, cleaning, and office) in a secure place that is inaccessible to participants and use non-toxic materials when possible to avoid endangering participants;

- ● minimize multiple sensory stimuli as much as possible to avoid adding to confusion;

● designate space for individuals needing to pace;

● provide a space for private moments for participants; and

● provide a secure outdoor area.

Evaluation

In addition to the Evaluation components of the overall standards, attention should be paid to these important indicators:

● input from family/caregivers on the quality of care

● input from family/caregivers on the participant's satisfaction and benefits

● input from family/caregivers on family/caregiver satisfaction and benefits, including changes in the family/caregiver situation

● consideration of the ability of the family/caregiver to work

● consideration of the ability to maintain the participant in the home and community

● review of the effect of combining participants with dementia with cognitively intact participants in an integrated program.

Profiles of Programs in Special Settings and Those That Serve Special Populations

Introduction

There are unique benefits and challenges to providing adult day care services in rural areas, just as there are in providing those services to a small group of adults in a residential setting. The first two profiles, therefore, offer guidance on tailoring this service and adapting the national standards to these two settings.

The other six profiles focus on adult day care programs for specialized populations. These profiles are included in order to convey the special needs and challenges of serving these individuals in order to help providers consider either expanding or focusing their target populations. The profiles address the special needs of the individuals and the adaptations necessary in adult day care.

The profiles of programs serving specialized populations include programs responding to those with: Rehabilitative Needs, Head Injury, Developmental Disabilities, AIDS, Sensory Impairments, and Mental Illness.

In addition to the resources included in most of the profiles, the authors of the profiles are identified and would welcome further inquiries into their areas of expertise. Their contribution to the standards-development project is sincerely appreciated.

Rural Adult Day Care

by Ruth Von Behren, Ph.D.

*Rural areas are unique. They differ from urban
areas in their geography, population density, economy,
lifestyle, values and social organization. Rural areas'
people require programs that respond to their unique
characteristics and needs rather than scaled-down
urban programs that do not consider rural differences.*
—Statement by the National Rural Health Association

Adult day care has been developed primarily in urban
areas. In California, for example, 32 of 58 counties do not
have even one adult day health care center. These counties
are predominantly rural with sparse scattered population,
geographic barriers, and a high percentage of seniors.
Being proposed is legislation that would establish a Rural
Alternative Adult Day Health Care Act. California's 1989
Senior Legislature has identified this as one of its top ten
priorities. It is needed because California's laws,
guidelines, rules, and regulations—designed for urban
settings—have constituted a barrier to rural service
development.

Rural Area

A universally accepted, useful definition does not exist.
The Census bureau generally says that any area with less
than 50,000 population is not a standard metropolitan

statistical area (SMSA). However, this definition can include rural farms and rural non-farms, as well as towns and cities over 50,000 persons, in an SMSA. "Non-metropolitan area" is, therefore, not the same as rural.

Rural areas are very diverse. A continuum exists that starts with what has been defined as "frontier" rural (six or less persons per square mile) and extends to larger rural communities serving as market place and government center for the surrounding area, which may even be adjacent to urban areas.

The major characteristic of rural areas is distance—long distance between houses and long stretches of space between towns and population clusters. Distance is compounded by poor roads and geographic barriers such as mountains, which make transportation difficult.

"Rural" means driving ten miles for a loaf of bread, forty-five miles to a hospital, sixty miles to deliver a home-delivered meal. Rural is living in a town where the only elevator is for corn, the only buses are for school children, and the only stoplight in the county is at the corner of Main and Highway 16. Rural is never having to worry about finding a parking place or locking your car.

Over one-third of the nation's older people live in rural communities. Elders form 25 percent of the total rural population, compared to 12 percent of the total U.S. population. This percentage is likely to increase due to out-migration of young people to work in urban areas and in-migration of older people who retire to a safer, cleaner, cheaper place.

Rural elders have a higher poverty rate, lower median income, and poorer health status than their urban counterparts. Problems with physical mobility and inadequate transportation make getting around difficult.

The rural economy has been significantly damaged by

the agricultural recession of the 1980s. Since 1980, the rural unemployment rate has been consistently higher than the urban rate—reversing an historical pattern. Areas with low population density dropped even lower with massive out-migration of rural residents. The lower tax base means lower public funds to support services. Federal funds have been disproportionately reduced in rural areas.

Service providers in rural areas have problems of service density and scale. Small numbers of people require a variety of services. Rural programs face productivity measures, administrative costs, and costs per unit of service based on experiences with larger urban programs, which benefit from economies of scale.

Hiring professional staff is a major problem in rural areas. Salaries and benefits are usually lower, and professionals fear professional isolation and a lack of opportunities for professional growth.

The recent staff report to the Senate Special Committee on Aging, "The Rural Health Care Challenge, 1988," suggests the need to examine state practice acts for their role in restricting the utilization and availability of health care personnel and encourages the development of generalists or multi-competency personnel, acknowledging the overlap between various health professions.

NIAD recognizes that the method of delivering adult day care in rural communities often needs to be different. Successful programs have built upon existing community resources, drawing upon components of the adult day care services from many different sources. One of the advantages of living in a rural area is the strong belief in cooperation and the willingness to work together to solve local problems. Innovation and creativity result when governmental barriers are removed. For example, "mobile" adult day care programs have been developed in which the professional staff travels to various centers and core staff remain at each center. Churches, schools, senior centers, American Legion halls, community centers—all have been utilized for sites, as have private residences. Satellite centers have been developed. The parent adult day care center is usually located in the area's largest community, with small satellite centers located in neighboring towns and sharing administration, staff, and services with the parent center.

Regulatory agencies need to state clearly what program services, staffing, and facility flexibilities are allowed in their adult day care requirements. Rural areas need to know the parameters of flexibility in order to develop economically feasible and participant-acceptable adult day care programs. Specific suggestions are stated below.

Administrative Structure And Organization

Recognizing that rural adult day care programs are likely to serve a small number of people (many will serve less than ten daily) and that a number of such centers may be needed, centralized administration, consortia, and joint public-private ventures should be encouraged. Administrative policies and procedures need to recognize the small scale of the program and not be overly burdensome.

Services

Utilizing existing services whenever possible, rural adult day care centers should provide—directly or indirectly and with the scope and intensity required by the needs of the participants—the essential core services of personal care, nursing, social services, therapeutic activities, nutrition, transportation, emergency plan, and education. Additional and other services may also be provided if available and needed.

Community resources should be utilized where feasible, as discussed below.

Staffing

Shortages of health and social work professionals are particularly acute in rural areas. In order to provide needed services in areas where persons meeting the NIAD standards are not available, the following suggestions are made:

● Share staff with other health and/or social service agencies. The public health nurse, county welfare social worker, and hospital physical therapist could all provide consultation, assessment, care planning, and general supervision of service provision.

● Utilize qualified volunteers, particularly retired persons. Many would be willing to commit the time needed.

● Encourage generalist staff roles and blur distinctions between disciplines.

● Increase the role and responsibilities of other professionals and paraprofessionals, such as licensed vocational or practical nurses and certified occupational or physical therapist assistants. Persons with such credentials and experience in working with adults with functional impairment are valuable additions to center staff.

● Substitute successful and relevant experience for educational credentials wherever persons with these credentials are not available. Many successful and highly respected community agencies have been administered by persons lacking academic degrees. Quality service delivery often arises as much from experience and on-the-job training as from academic courses. In California, for example, there are counties in which no one has a master's degree in social work—yet social services are and have been provided.

● Work to change restrictive state practices acts and other laws and regulations that are barriers to rural service delivery. Design programs that will address the needs and circumstances of rural living described in the beginning of this profile.

Facility

Finding appropriate space—a place not requiring extensive renovation for an adult day care program that may meet several days per week to serve only eight people—is often a problem.

In small communities, the most appropriate local place may be a hospital or a nursing home. Advantages are that resources such as meals, staff (nurses, social workers, and therapists), activities, and equipment are often there. Co-location should be encouraged and sharing allowed, except for a multi-purpose room devoted exclusively to adult day care. Participants need a place to call "home," although meals and some services may be provided elsewhere in the building.

Use of buildings primarily built for other purposes (and often still used for the original purpose at different times) means a need for flexibility in facility standards. Such sites may include, for example, Sunday school rooms, private homes, church social halls, community centers, and Legion Halls.

Adult day care programs have been provided successfully in such settings for years. The therapeutic milieu does not always depend on the physical setting. Make the center as safe, accessible, attractive, and enjoyable as possible, and put your emphasis on service delivery.

Evaluation

Rural adult day care providers will also benefit from self-evaluation. Determine what is applicable and appropriate for your circumstances. Informal community evaluation may help in the formal evaluation. External monitoring by funding and licensing agencies also provides perspective on program quality.

Summary

Putting together the components of adult day care in a rural area demands strong community support, use of informal networks, and a willingness to meet the program goals in innovative ways. The need is there.

RURAL RESOURCE LIST

The National Center on Rural Aging (NCRA)
The National Council on the Aging
600 Maryland Avenue, SW, West Wing 100
Washington, DC. 20024
(202) 479-1200
   Regarded as the national clearinghouse on rural aging concerns, NCRA
offers information and technical assistance on rural issues affecting older
adults. This constituent unit of NCOA focuses national attention on the special
needs of older persons in rural areas, and spotlights successful rural aging
programs.

Other national organizations

National Rural Health Association
301 East Armour Boulevard, Suite 420
Kansas City, MO 64111
(816) 756-3140

University of Missouri—Kansas City
National Resource Center for Rural Elderly
5100 Rockhill Road
Kansas City, MO 64110-2499

References

Benn, Darla R., *Accessing Existing Resources to Develop a Community-Based Adult Day Care Program in a Rural Community.* Lewistown, Pa.: Mifflin-Juniata Area Agency on Aging, Inc., 1984. Available from Mifflin-Juniata Area Agency on Aging, Inc., P.O. Box 750, Lewistown, Pennsylvania 17044.

Blaser, C. Jean, Ph.D. and P.L. Gunter, Ph.D., *A Mobile Model: Handbook for Developing a Rural Adult Day Care Program, Volume 2.* Carbondale, Ill.: Southern Illinois University at Carbondale, 1985. Available from C. Jean Blaser, Ph.D., Manager, Division of Long-Term Care, Illinois Department on Aging, 421 East Capitol Avenue, Springfield, Illinois 62701. ($2.50)

California Senate, "Barriers to Providing Long-Term Care in Rural Areas," Hearing before Subcommittee on Aging, Gilroy, Calif. Nov. 16, 1987.

Sacramento, Calif.: Joint Publications, 1987, State Capitol Box 942849, Sacramento, CA 94249-0001. ($8)

Cohen, Saul, M.S., S. McDermott, M.P.H., J. Smith, L.S.W. and D. Laonies, *Adult Residential Day Care: A Program Development and Operations Guide*. Boise, Idaho: Mountain State Health Corporation, 1984. Available from Mountain States Health Corporation, 1303 W. Fort Street, P.O. Box 6756, Boise, Idaho. ($12)

Gunter, P.L., "Rural Adult Day Care means Nontraditional Delivery," *Perspective on Aging*, NCOA, Special Issue, Adult Day Care in the United States. Washington, D.C.: National Council on the Aging, Inc. November-December 1985. p.8.

U.S. Congress, Senate, Special Committee on Aging, "The Rural Health Care Challenge," Staff Report to the Special Committee on Aging. Washington, D.C.: U.S. Government Printing Office. U. S. Senate, Serial No. 100-N, October 1988.

Residential Adult Day Care

by Ruth Von Behren, Ph.D.

The site for delivery of adult day care is sometimes a private residence also used as a primary residence by the provider. Adult day care homes, residential adult day care, and family adult day care are terms used when the service site is the provider's home.

Residential adult day care exists in a number of states. Other states are investigating its feasibility. Although often the same regulations are used for residential and non-residential adult day care, some states, such as North Carolina, New Mexico, North Dakota, and Hawaii, have acknowledged the special characteristics of residential adult day care by making specific exemptions to adult day care center requirements or by developing separate regulations. A two-year demonstration project with separate requirements is underway in Maryland. Past demonstration projects utilizing adult day care homes have taken place in Idaho and Pennsylvania.

Residential adult day care has the same philosophy and objectives as adult day care provided in a center. Choice of a residence as the site of service delivery is usually influenced by the following reasons.

● Serving a sparse, scattered target population over a large area (often accompanied by geographic barriers) makes transportation difficult, time consuming, and costly. A number of very small day care programs may be needed, to provide access for adults with impairments and to minimize transportation costs. A private residence provides appropriate space and is most likely to be available where population clusters are.

● Persons, particularly those with dementia or depression, who cannot adapt to a large group program may find the home setting and the small group more acceptable.

Special consideration in adult day care standards must be given to residential day care in order for this form of care to become a feasible and vital part of the adult day care continuum of services. NIAD recommends that regulatory authorities recognize areas of differences in developing adult day care program standards.

In states where licensing is required for adult day care centers, it should also be required for adult day care homes, with exceptions and flexibilities clearly identified. Adult day care homes should also have the opportunity to qualify for Medicaid or other certification with appropriate exceptions or flexibility identified.

Areas of difference follow.

● Adult day care is provided in a private residence, built to meet housing codes, not in a building designed for public occupancy.

● The program is small in size. The appropriate size is from two to no more than five adults.

● The provider is likely to be a nonprofessional or a paraprofessional. Therefore, the standards must be modified while quality is preserved.

● Service provision will vary depending upon the participant's needs and community resources.

The NIAD standards are discussed below with recommended exceptions for residential adult day care.

Target Population

Residential adult day care serves the same target population as an adult day care center. In determining appropriateness for residential adult day care, the "provider" will need to consider his or her qualifications, the qualifications of other staff, consultants, or volunteers, and the home's accessibility to those with handicaps. In states where licensing or certification is required, an assessment of the home and prospective provider is usually done by a professional nurse or social worker as part of the licensing process. If case management is used, either of these professionals should make the referrals.

Administration And Organization

Residential adult day care may be a single site owned by the provider, a satellite for an adult day care center, or one site among several day care homes operated by a parent agency.

Advantages to being part of a larger organization include: greater resources to draw upon; the ability to share professional staff; peer support; and sharing of administrative, fiscal, personnel, and support services and responsibilities. Existing centers may find that the addition of a day care home or two enables them to expand their services in an area that would not economically support a larger center.

The administrative and organizational standards apply to adult day care homes that are part of a larger organization. In the case of sole proprietorship, the requirement for a formal governing body does not apply. All other *standards* apply; however it is recognized that some *recommendations* may not apply and that compliance may be a simplified version of the standard. Monitoring agencies should use common sense in determining the appropriate degree of compliance.

Services

The essential components of intake screening, pre-admission assessment, professional assessment (rather than a team assessment), and the professional development of an individual plan should be carried out in residential adult day care. How this is done and by whom will vary according to the organizational structure and affiliation of the day care home. Consultants, parent agency professionals, public agency nurses, and/or social workers may be involved as well as the provider, appropriate staff, the participant, family, and the participant's physician.

Although it is recognized that the scale or intensity of services will vary, residential adult day care must provide the essential core services of personal care, nursing, social services, therapeutic activities, nutrition and therapeutic diets, transportation, emergency services, and education. Use of community resources and consultants is strongly recommended. Unless the provider is a licensed vocational nurse, licensed practical nurse, or a registered nurse, provision of nursing services will be limited.

The provider should be responsible for the following services, under the guidance of a professional nurse:

● observation of the participant(s), including daily documentation of information regarding attendance hours, medical appointments, outings, assistance given in personal care and activities of daily living, changes in the participant's functional and health status, adherence to the medical regimen, and other observations as he/she deems necessary or as requested by the physician or primary caregiver;

● monitoring vital signs and weight;

● liaison with the participant's personal physician, notifying him/her of changes in health status;

● assistance with activities of daily living including assistance (when needed) for increasing or maintaining independence in activities of daily living such as bathing, toileting, feeding, walking, and dressing, including the use of adaptive equipment or environmental aids;

● supervision of the self-administration of prescribed medication and documentation of medication taken by the participant. Consultant nursing services are essential.

Although the provider may utilize a consultant social worker on a part-time basis, the provider should be responsible for maintaining communication with the participants, families, and other service providers involved in the care of the participant for the purpose of solving day-to-day problems. Standards of additional and other services apply to adult day care homes if they choose to include these services.

The provider also needs a plan for emergency medical services. This should include the name and telephone

number of each participant's physician and an agreement
with a physician to provide emergency care. The plan must
also include ambulance procedures or a procedure for
calling 911 for any life-threatening situation.

Staffing

The small size of the adult day care home will influence
staffing requirements. This area will deviate substantially
from NIAD standards.

Emphasis will be on the qualifications of the adult day
care home provider. Minimum qualifications for the adult
day care home provider require that he or she:

● be twenty-one years or older;

● be competent and qualified to carry out the
responsibilities of an adult day care program;

● have, at minimum, a high school education or the
equivalent;

● have at least two years of full-time work experience
in services to the elderly and/or adults with
handicaps and demonstrated ability to manage all
aspects of a day care program;

● provide a written statement from a physician or a
physician's assistant certifying good health,
including freedom from communicable disease, prior
to beginning the day care program and annually
thereafter. [Note: With a requirement for a case
manager to do training and monitoring of the
provider, work experience with the target population
is not necessary. The case manager can determine if

the person's personality, character, and life experiences qualify him or her.];

● provide a written statement from a physician or a physician's assistant certifying good health, including freedom from communicable disease, prior to beginning the day care program and annually thereafter;

● have current Cardio-Pulmonary Resuscitation Training with renewals as frequently as required;

● have current First Aid Training Certification, to be renewed every three years;

● have the ability to work with people;

● have liability insurance coverage sufficient to protect the provider in case of an accident involving all participants at one time.

The licensing or monitoring agency should conduct a background investigation including: a criminal record check on the provider and home residents for a history of behavior potentially harmful to participants; a verification of past employment; and a references check.

Mandatory continuing education requirements are strongly recommended for all residential adult day care staff. Courses should include: the purpose of residential adult day care; overview of the aging process; how to make the home secure, comfortable, and safe for the participant(s); personal care and transfer procedures; nutrition; record-keeping; observation and recognition of significant signs and symptoms; therapeutic activities and appropriate exercises; handling emergencies; needs of the elderly; types of disabilities; and working with individuals with cognitive impairments.

Ideal qualifications for an adult day care home provider would be a person qualifying as a licensed vocational nurse, licensed practical nurse, home health aide, or certified nursing assistant.

Staffing Ratio

Adult day care homes usually have one staff person, the provider or home resident who combines administrative and program functions, drawing on community resources, consultants, or a parent agency to meet program requirements. The use of volunteers is strongly advised to enable the presence of two responsible persons at all times the participants are present.

One individual in a full-time equivalent staff position should have responsibility for direct participant care for no more than five participants. This staffing ratio should be maintained at all times. If the provider is the only staff, the day care home should have available a list of two readily available and qualified substitutes to cover any absences. In determining the staffing ratio, consideration should be given to the presence in the home of a baby or toddler who may need the provider's care. Community resources such as adult education, community colleges, arts and crafts teachers, and local musicians can be used to enhance the activities program and provide education.

Professional consultation for nursing and social services is necessary for residential adult day care programs.

Facility

The adult day care home should not be expected to meet all of the standards for an adult day care facility. Applicable state and local building regulations, zoning, fire, and health codes for private residences should be used—*not* the requirements for public occupancy. This means that adult day care homes may have, for example, normal residential heating systems and are exempt from meeting all state and local regulations governing food establishments.

As a private residence, the adult day care home enjoys certain advantages: it already has a kitchen, a bathroom including a shower or tub, laundry appliances, and furniture. A well-maintained house should meet the building requirements with minor changes such as the addition of grab bars or fire extinguishers.

Many of NIAD's facility standards can be adapted to adult day care homes, keeping in mind the differences. Facility standards have been developed by North Dakota, North Carolina, Maryland, and New Mexico, and may be obtained from those states.

The adult day care home will share space with the home's residents. A bedroom will probably serve as the quiet area and may be the room where nursing services are provided. The living room or family room may be the multipurpose area. Meals may be served there, or in the kitchen or dining room. In order to preserve the home atmosphere, customary use of household space should be maintained.

Adequate space (excluding hallways, closets, and bathrooms) should be available and be designated for participants.

Porches and steps must be protected by handrails.

The adult day care home must utilize the ground floor for its program unless participants can handle stairs. If persons in wheelchairs and those with handicaps are accepted, the home must provide ramps or other appropriate means of accessibility for those persons.

Adult day care homes must have at least one toilet and lavatory that may be used by either men or women as the conventional home bathroom is. A back-up commode such as a second toilet or bedside commode should be available. Grab bars must be provided for one toilet. Formal call bell systems are not needed—a hand bell can serve the same purpose.

Safety and sanitation requirements for homes should be required. The home and its premises must be clean, neat, and free from hazards that jeopardize health and safety. The house must be equipped with adequate light, heat, ventilation, and plumbing for safe and comfortable occupancy.

Safe storage of medications, toxic substances, trash, and garbage should be practiced.

Basic fire safety rules should be followed: no accumulation of highly combustible material in closets, basements, attics, or garages; appropriate screening of fireplaces and steam radiators; periodic inspection of heating units and fireplaces; the presence of smoke detectors and a five-pound class "ABC" all-purpose fire extinguisher, installed on the advice of the fire department; initial and periodic fire and safety checks by the fire department; safe storage of flammable liquids and chemicals; and appropriate use of fuses.

The adult day care home provider should post by each telephone the numbers of police, fire, and ambulance. Exit routes should be posted and staff and participants trained on how to exit and how to respond to the alarm.

The adult day care home should have at least two means of exit. Each should be at least thirty inches wide, and one exit should be a door providing direct access to the outside at street or ground level.

Household pets should have required shots.

Common sense and reasonable requirements, taking into account the nature of the building and the small size of the program, should be utilized by monitoring agencies.

Evaluation

A formal evaluation for a sole proprietorship adult day care home is best conducted by an outside monitoring agency that either funds or licenses the facility. The provider could use the NIAD *Self-Assessment Workbook* informally, when its items are appropriate, to ascertain areas where improvements are needed.

Conclusion

Adult day care homes make adult day care available and accessible to adults with impairments in areas where an adult day care center is not feasible. It should be considered a part of the richness and variety of the adult day care continuum of services. The nature of the service site should be acknowledged in appropriate standards.

Physical Rehabilitation-Oriented Adult Day Care Centers

by John Ashton, R.P.T., Clay Marcusen, R.N., B.S.N., and Linda Cook Webb, M.S.G.

Rehab-oriented adult day care typically serves people with heavy health care needs and complicated service requirements. This level of care is appropriate for those who need more constant care than can be provided through outpatient or home care programs and yet who elect community-based care over in-patient care (nursing home or hospital).

A common participant scenario is an overweight, 62-year-old man who has recently been discharged from the hospital, after a stroke. Complications may include some paralysis, aphasia, exaggerated emotional responses, hypertension, diabetes, history of smoking, multiple medications, and special diet. His wife is too small to help him in and out of the bathtub, and besides, the wheelchair won't fit through the bathroom door. She has recently started working, as his pension will not begin for another three years. He is depressed because he feels he is "not a man" and angry because he "didn't ask for this."

The adult day care center that focuses on physical rehabilitation must, by its nature, provide a high degree of professional services. In the example above, physical therapy (PT), occupational therapy (OT), speech therapy, nursing, and medical social services are all needed. At the same time, though, most day centers emphasizing rehabilitation will find it advisable to incorporate a component of maintenance-level care. This happens for two reasons.

● First, most communities do not have a concentrated population of persons needing rehabilitative care. It may, therefore, be difficult to justify a center serving exclusively those persons who can benefit from formal physical, occupational, or speech therapy. There may, however, be numerous persons who would benefit from the rehab milieu without participating in formal therapy.

● Second, some rehab patients in the program may complete their course of therapy and still be unable to graduate to sheltered employment or other community services. It can be quite appropriate to allow them to continue in adult day care for nursing supervision, socialization, and occasional "refresher" therapy.

Because there is frequently a combination of participants who are in formal therapy and those who are not, it is crucial to make certain that participants, families, staff, and volunteers understand the plan of care for each individual. Under no circumstances should there be confusion regarding which participants are to be involved in formal therapy and which are not. At the same time, many families will prefer the strong goal-orientation of a rehabilitation day care center even for their family member who cannot benefit from therapy treatment. As long as care plans are clear, both groups can be served well.

The following comments pertain *only* to the rehabilitation aspects of a multiple-service adult day care center. Remember that they must be balanced with the needs of, and services to, participants who are not in treatment.

The goals of physical rehabilitation services in adult day care will center around improvement of the participant's functioning in ADLs (mobility, dressing, eating, etc.) and IADLs (shopping, cooking, using the phone, etc.). Some rehab patients will eventually move on to employment, other community services, or simply more independent living. Others will benefit from long-term supervision in the day care center, to encourage slow but persistent progress or to prevent regression of function.

Establishing eligibility of particular rehab patients must be done by an interdisciplinary team. The applicable therapist(s) should determine whether formal therapy is likely to be effective. A nurse should review medical, nursing, and health teaching needs. Eligibility criteria should also include reference to the patient's motivation and mental status, as well as the family's ability to follow through at home. While the therapists and nurse can assess these factors, it is preferable for a medical social worker to do so.

As the general standards state, this type of day care should have a higher than average staffing ratio. Professional therapists are likely to be at the center half-time or less, and therefore will not be counted in the ratio. Among full-time staff, it is advisable to include Certified Occupational Therapy Assistants (COTAs) and Physical Therapy Assistants (PTAs). This will maximize the benefit of professional time available and will allow assistance with or supervision of exercises during the entire day. It is advisable that the nurse in a rehabilitation-oriented center be a full-time Registered Nurse (RN). Depending on the direct care nursing needs of rehab patients, it may also be advisable to utilize Licensed Practical or Vocational Nurses (LPNs or LVNs) and Certified Nurse Aides (CNAs) to supplement RN services. Staff not counted in the ratio (secretary, janitor, etc.) should also be given special training to allow them to respond appropriately in interactions with participants in therapy. It is important that everyone approaches the day with a rehab philosophy. As in any day care center, team work is of the essence!

Specialized services available in a rehab-oriented adult day care center include all those described in the Standards, Part Three: Services, Standards 83, 84, and 85. It can also be expected that rehabilitation patients will need at least some of the nursing services outlined in that section. In addition, the following are common rehabilitation-related day care services.

● Therapy exercises can be incorporated in center activities. Therapists and nurses often consult with the activities coordinator in developing or modifying activities.

● Observing participants throughout the day is a means of collecting additional informal assessment information. This service is often performed for participants who are not involved in therapy, to determine if a full assessment is indicated or to provide feedback during case conferences.

● Inspecting used or worn equipment to determine essential repairs or adjustments may be necessary, as may be making minor repairs or adjustments and referring for major repairs.

● They may be procedures that require cooperation between nursing and therapy, such as stump wrapping to prepare an amputated limb for a new prosthesis.

● Some rehabilitation-oriented centers even specialize in rehab nursing procedures such as continence restoration. In this case, a patient may be admitted primarily for rehabilitation nursing and only secondarily for PT or OT services.

● Cardiac rehabilitation, employing nursing and therapy, is a "natural" for day care.

● Laboratory services are often needed. Some, such as checking blood-sugar, can be performed on-site. For others, center staff should be able to draw blood to send to an off-site lab.

● Hydrotherapy (whirlpool) is a critical therapy service, but nursing can also use the equipment for treatment of decubitus ulcers.

● Bathing is more necessary in rehab day centers than other types, due to frequent physical limitations in the home.

Adequate facilities and equipment are quite important to the success of a rehabilitation-oriented center. In addition to the specifications outlined in the standards, the following should be considered.

● Varying surfaces (vinyl flooring, carpet, brick, stone, etc.) as well as steps should be included in the center design, to allow a fuller range of gait training experiences. Note that these surfaces and steps should not be located so as to present a barrier to any participant.

● A small teaching kitchen with adaptive devices is helpful. This can be a part of the kitchen used to serve the center's lunches.

● Bathing should be done in a shower that is large enough to be entered by two persons at one time. The shower head should be hand-held, with an adaptation for wall mounting. There should be a dressing area with mirrors nearby. The shower area should be somewhat warmer than the rest of the facility, and have separate thermostat control.

● A hydraulic patient lift may be a temporary necessity for persons who have just been admitted from the hospital.

The rehabilitation-oriented adult day care center may become certified as a Medicare provider of outpatient therapy. In this case, there will be specific regulations that the center must meet.

Resource

Rehabilitation services are discussed in the book edited by one of the Profile authors, Linda Cook Webb, *Planning and Managing Adult Day Care*—see the Resources section of this publication.

Adult Day Care Serving Participants with Head Injuries

*by Linda Cook Webb, M.S.G.,
Dennis Swiercinsky, Ph.D., and Phyllis Snyder*

Many head-injured persons complete the acute phase of their rehabilitation and still need some type of continued stabilization. Some may need two to three years of therapy before being able to resume their accustomed life style. Others may never return to school or work, but still need to find a positive focus in their lives.

The adult day care center may be able to offer these people a unique combination of continued rehabilitation, behavior management, and a positive long-term milieu. Adult day care does not have to limit length of stay or admit only those persons with potential to re-enter competitive employment (as some other outpatient services might). It therefore has the advantage of being able to provide the long-term treatment and support so important to this special population. It will be necessary, however, to understand the needs of head-injured participants and to provide particular services that address their life situation.

Persons who have sustained head injuries can range from a child hit by a car to a mature worker injured on the job. The head trauma patients seen in adult day care, though, often have sustained their injury during a traffic accident in which alcohol was involved. They are frequently in their early 20s, and may have social histories showing that they are high risk-takers with marginal personal relationships. In fact, in some cases, it may be a long-standing inadequate support system combined with the head injury that leads to the need for adult day care.

Whatever the reason for the original injury, persons with head trauma often face a combination of physical, cognitive, and emotional limitations. When they reach adult day care, they may still experience some paralysis, limited motor control, aphasia, memory loss, poor judgment, impaired conversational skills, inappropriate social behaviors, low self-esteem, motivation problems, and emotional dyscontrol. They will also bring with them all the problems they may have had before the accident. Poor social skills, substance abuse, and personality disorder may all play a part in participation at day care. In addition, younger participants will continue to go through the normal development processes appropriate to their age. Their concerns about dating, sexuality, jobs, privacy, and independence may seem to be quite different from the concerns of older participants. For these reasons, it may be wise to concentrate special activities for the head-injured on two or three days a week.

Many of the services beneficial to the head-injured population will be the same as, or will blend easily with, the services offered to all participants. Others should be specialized to the needs of head-injured persons.

As the standards state, all day care participants should receive an initial evaluation and periodic re-assessment, both resulting in an individual care plan. This process is especially important for persons with head trauma, as their progress may be long and slow. Specific reassessments encourage the staff to notice small gains.

Since many of the participants with head injury may be completing a course of physical rehabilitation, it will be important to offer physical and occupational therapy services. Speech therapy may be indicated for cognitive remediation and to work with persons experiencing aphasia. Nursing supervision will be important to those participants who may be taking anti-convulsive or other medications. For further discussion of these services, see the profile on "Physical Rehabilitation-Oriented Adult Day Care Centers."

Providing environmental cues and memory aides will be important to some persons with head trauma. Depending on the individual's prognosis, memory games and logic games may also be helpful. The guidance of professional staff or consultants should be sought in developing these activities.

Many participants with head trauma will benefit from practice in basic social skills. Discussion groups can be used to help develop communication abilities, such as staying "on the point" and listening to others. Encouraging participants to share personal histories and to take an interest in each other can support developing friendships. Staff may have to be creative in one-to-one suggestions for how to offer and receive friendly gestures. Staff should be particularly sensitive in dealing with romantic and sexual attractions between participants. The elderly participants can be of great help in supporting the development of social skills. Some, in befriending younger participants, may take a quasi-grandparent role. Others may be extremely clear in their disapproval of certain inappropriate behaviors.

The program should specifically include activities designed to develop judgment skills. Some discussion groups can focus on an individual's behavioral options and the consequences of his/her actions. This technique can be used to develop a regular, specialized activity, discussing "Situations, Options, and Consequences" or it can be consciously included in other discussions, such as newspaper reading. Activities that encourage setting and working toward personal goals can be helpful as well.

Behavior monitoring and management will be an important component. Some head-injured persons have difficulty dealing with multiple or strong stimuli. As the environment becomes more charged, these participants may become agitated, physically act out, or verbally abuse others. The center should be able to provide a milieu calming to these people, yet stimulating enough to be interesting. There should also be a range of stimulus level, to gently challenge those who are able to improve. A simple way to provide this continuum is to arrange spaces from which individuals can watch activities without participating. If the person is able to tolerate this, he/she could be encouraged to "just sit with the group for a while" with the understanding that leaving the group will also be accepted. If some activities are predictably loud or active or emotional, it might be advisable to have a volunteer do one-to-one activities with the individual in another room during those times. In assessing the continuum of stimuli, it will also be important to look at colors, lighting, general sound levels, and so forth, throughout the center.

Vocational services can be incorporated in the program, through participant volunteering. Folding cancer bandages or applying mailing labels for other community agencies are often favorite activities. Some participants may even progress to volunteering or sheltered employment in the community. Some centers include sheltered workshop as a service. Since this is often a state-regulated activity, it is wise to research the requirements and costs.

Developing daily living skills is of great importance to many head-injured persons. Practicing making change, balancing a checkbook, shopping, making a "to do" list, and similar activities can become a specialized part of the program. Often, the support of a small group that is relearning the same skills can be helpful.

Education regarding head injury will be important not only to the participants with this diagnosis, but also to their families, and even to the other participants in the center. Everyone involved may need to understand why memory, judgment, and behavior are affected the way they are.

As the general standards state, this type of day care should have a higher than average staffing ratio. In addition, the center should arrange for part-time physical, occupational, and speech therapists. An outside professional consultant, preferably a neuropsychologist or rehabilitation psychologist, strongly versed in overall behavioral treatment of head injury is highly advisable. Ideally, this person would provide staff training and participate in case conferences. As with any adult day care center, all staff should be empathetic and flexible.

It will be especially important to link into related programs through other community agencies. Support groups organized through the National Head Injury Foundation can be particularly effective in providing information and advocacy opportunities for families and center staff.

For Further Reading

Natinal Head Injury Foundation, *Catalogue of Educational Materials.* Southborough, Mass.: National Head Injury Foundation, 1989.

Swiercinsky, Dennis P., T.L. Price, and L.E. Leaf, *Traumatic Brain Injury: Cause, Consequence, and Challenge.* Shawnee Mission, Kans.: Kansas Head Injury Association, 1987.

Warrington, Jeanette, *The Humpty Dumpty Syndrome*. Southborough, Mass.: National Head Injury Foundation, 1981.

Resources

Kansas Head Injury Association, 9401 Nole #105, Shawnee Mission, KS 66207. 1-913-648-4772.

National Head Injury Foundation, 333 Turnpike Road, Southborough, MA 01772. 1-508-485-9950.

Profile on Mental Retardation and Developmental Disabilities

by Matthew P. Janicki, Ph.D.

The overriding feature of older persons with a developmental disability is that they are people first, older persons second, and individuals with some limitations due to their lifelong disability third. Programs serving older persons with special needs need to be aware that they should endeavor to ensure that their users remain as much a part of their community as possible and that both physical and social integration are integral aspects of each program's therapeutic goals.

Congress recognized the special needs of older persons with mental retardation and other developmental disabilities when it passed the Older Americans Act Amendments of 1987 (*PL 100-175*). Special provisions were included for "*individuals with disabilities*" which include persons with developmental disabilities. These provisions recognize the special needs of older persons with disabilities and call for closer collaboration and coordination of services between the aging network and disability agencies and the inclusion of persons with life-long disabilities within the gamut of special services available and provided to needy older persons.

What are "developmental disabilities"?

The term "*developmental disabilities*" encompasses a variety of conditions that originated at birth or in childhood. These can include autism, cerebral palsy, epilepsy, mental retardation, learning disabilities, and other similar neurological impairments. None of these disabilities are a mental illness or a disease. Instead, they constitute a lifelong mental or physical impairment that became apparent during childhood and has hampered an individual's ability to participate in mainstream society, either socially or vocationally. In addition, some people with one disability, such as mental retardation, can also have another disability, such as seizures (epilepsy) or motor dysfunction (cerebral palsy).

The best way to understand a *developmental* disability is to think of it as a condition an individual has had since birth or childhood, which has prevented him or her from being socially or vocationally fully independent as an adult and which is expected to continue into old age.

Developmental disabilities may:

● cause an adult to be slower in their thinking or less agile in their movements;

● be associated with impaired speech or social judgment; and

● also be, when severe, associated with other impediments such as seizures or impaired movement, and deficits in sensory, language, and social abilities.

Such disabilities are important to identify and understand during childhood and adolescence, since much

can be done to aid persons to work around the disability.
With old age, such considerations are less important since
the pressures of work and competition are minimal.
Impairments associated with these lifelong disabilities
mirror, in many ways, the impairments evident in seniors
with late-life disabilities, and with old age diagnosis of a
developmental disability is less clinically important.

Mental retardation, the most prevalent developmental
disability, is defined as subaverage intellectual functioning
that originates during the developmental period and is
associated with impairments in adaptive behavior.

● Persons with mental retardation characteristically
   have limited ability to learn and difficulty in using
   what they have learned.

● Mental retardation has a variety of causes, including
   problems associated with premature birth, genetic
   abnormalities, malnutrition, exposure to toxic agents,
   or social and environmental deprivation.

● The degree of mental retardation varies greatly from
   person to person. Although one individual may be
   fully integrated within the mainstream of society,
   another individual who is more disabled may always
   require some degree of supervision. Most people
   with mental retardation are capable of learning to
   care for themselves and to function in society.

With advanced age, older persons with mental
retardation generally experience the same rate of physical
and medical problems as other seniors. Contrary to some
beliefs, persons with mental retardation do not normally
age earlier than other age peers of the same cultural or
socioeconomic background. One exception is among
persons with Down syndrome, a prevalent cause of mental

retardation. Persons with Down syndrome do age earlier (usually by about 20 years) and have a greater incidence of Alzheimer's disease (about one out of every three older persons).

Characteristics of the Population

Estimates of the size of the population of older persons with developmental disabilities in the United States begin usually at about 200,000 or about 4 out of every 1000 older individuals. The number of older Americans with a developmental disability has increased in size, as well as visibility, and will continue to grow in the years to come. Changes in health care, nutrition, early childhood services, and social and housing conditions have led to decreases in mortality and morbidity and increases in the survivor rate of persons with such lifelong disabilities. Expectations are that these trends will continue, particularly given the confluence of federal statutes promoting enriched programs, service entitlements, and general overall improved health status.

In terms of this older population, the National Institute on Aging report, "*Personnel for the Health Needs of the Elderly in the Year 2020,*" identified three major groups, each with a different demand upon day or support services:

● The *first* group is generally made up of those individuals with *minimal mental or physical handicap* who have been fairly independent all their adult lives, and only because of impairments associated with aging have they again become dependent upon special assistance from social services agencies or the aging network.

● The *second* group is made up of those individuals with *moderate cognitive or physical impairments*, who have a need for supervision or special training, and who as they age become more dependent upon a range of special mental retardation/developmental disabilities, social services, and aging network services. These are the individuals most likely to be recommended for admission to adult day care services.

● The *third* group is made up of those individuals with *severe or profound cognitive and/or physical impairments*, whose gross dependency calls for a range of very specialized long-term care and habilitation services, and who have been the life-long responsibility of mental retardation/developmental disabilities agencies and for the most part will remain so as they age.

Reasons for Referral

Persons with a developmental disability will be referred to adult day care programs for several reasons:

● one, problems inherent in *two-generation-elderly families* in which an elderly parent (or parents) who has continued to bear the burden of care for an aging adult son or daughter with a developmental disability finally finds that he/she needs respite or other assistance;

● second, problems related to *"aging in place"* of older adults with developmental disabilities currently living in a variety of community residential situations (such as foster family care homes, group homes, board and care homes, supportive apartments, and the like) and who, to prevent unnecessary institutionalization, need a change in the types of services provided;

● third, realizations within small communities that *duplicative day services are expensive* and counterproductive. Consequently, local health or aging officials may be looking to consolidate day services for age-similar dependent populations with common needs operated by different human service agencies. This would mean that existing adult day care programs that may only take in individuals with age-related impairments, may need to open their doors to age peers with lifelong disabilities who require equivalent care. Conversely, disability providers who run adult day care-type programs may be encouraged to broaden their user base and serve persons with age-associated impairments with similar care needs.

Most of the seniors with a developmental disability who use adult day care reside in either community residences or foster family care homes operated under the aegis of mental retardation/developmental disabilities agencies; however, a smaller, albeit growing, number also come from their family homes.

Characteristics of Programs

Unlike participants at nutrition sites and senior centers, who tend to be "*well*" elderly, those attending adult day care programs are typically persons who have impairments that limit their activities of daily living. In this regard, persons with developmental disabilities who may be users of adult day care share many similarities with other clientele served at day care sites. They may have physical impairments that limit their speech, mobility, or range of motion; they may have cognitive limitations that limit their capability to be fully independent in activities of daily living; or they simply may need supervision because of limited judgment or lack of independent survival abilities. In instances where medical or behavioral management needs are pronounced they will remain the responsibility of disability agencies and be provided for in specialized settings.

Initial screening for day care site admissions should be based upon how well functional ability and behavior, rather than the nature of disability, coincides with that of the participants already enrolled in the program. Since day care programming takes place in a social environment, individuals considered for integration should have the potential to adapt to a social setting and not have problem behaviors or be a danger to themselves or others. Programming at day care sites is usually paced to an older, more dependent, population so persons selected should be matched to the same activity level occurring at the site.

Adult day care programs that have a minimal health care component are similar in many respects to the day activity, training or habilitation programs operated for adults by agencies serving persons with a developmental disability. Because of these similarities, many older adults with a developmental disability can readily adapt to day care settings and programs. Admission is usually facilitated when operators meet the individual being referred, and determine the extent of similarity with existing users, and offer them a period of time to visit the program and acclimate to the setting.

Conversely, adult day care programs with a strong health component are similar to the types of services often found in developmental disabilities program settings funded under state Medicaid programs. Standards and program practices focus more on training and provision of *"therapies"* and health-related services. The individuals served are generally more impaired and in need of specialized and individualized care services directed by a team of providers following the prescriptions of an individualized treatment plan.

When considering admitting persons with a developmental disability into an existing day care program, thought should be given to the following:

● the functional abilities of the persons to be admitted should be reasonably the same as other participants;

● the program's expectation should be gone over with the individual so he/she will know what to expect from the program; and

● the referring agency should be solicited for information about any particularities in behavior that the individual may have.

Staffing in programs operated by disability agencies is generally richer than typical aging network programs. However, staff of both types of programs should receive cross-training in aging and disability issues and topics, including aging and special needs of elderly persons, nutrition and health practices, recreational activities, counseling, effects of disabilities, communication skills with non-verbal or speech-impaired seniors, basic first aid, and behavioral intervention and observation techniques.

Program Adaptations

The program content within a particular site will vary; however the common theme should be that persons with a developmental disability should be able to choose from a range of activities offered in a relaxed and comfortable atmosphere.

Program components should contain: health and sensory concern features; recreation and physical fitness; a variety of activities to stimulate cognitive skills, range of motion, socialization, and creativity; and individual or group counseling. Attention to health care concerns and observance of physical and sensory limitations, and nutrition information should be part of the program. Recreation activities should include community trips to museums, zoos, plays, historical or other sites of interest, and parks. Within the programs, recreation activities should offer a range of involvements, from cooking projects and gardening, to crafts and hobbies. The program activities designed for seniors with a developmental disability are generally similar to activities provided to other seniors.

In some instances, participants with a developmental disability may also be attending, on a part-time basis, a sheltered workshop or other type of work program and the day care program needs to be sensitive to the distinctions in the demands of each of the settings.

Persons with a late-life disability may be in need of adult day care for wholly different reasons than persons with a lifelong disability, consequently adjustment to the routines and expectations among these two groups may vary. The programmatic features of typical developmental disabilities programs may produce expectations among users with developmental disabilities for behavior that may be both dysfunctional and complimentary to the setting:

● As with other age peers who have been fairly independent all their lives, to avoid dysfunction problems, allow the individual to slowly acclimate to a different set of programmatic demands and thus be gradually introduced to new and interesting activities as a means of aiding adjustment.

● Many older individuals with a developmental disability have spent some portion of their lives in institutional or highly structured settings and adjustment to adult day care can be quite positive— that is, they are used to such settings. Because of this, persons with developmental disabilities are generally less impaired than other seniors with late-life disabilities and often can serve in "volunteer" roles by helping their age-peers.

Because many older adults with a developmental disability referred to an adult day care program were previously enrolled in work-age programs that were designed to provide constant involvement and training, little time was generally devoted to free time or self-exploratory activities. Anecdotally, adult day care program operators have noted that seniors with a developmental disability "blossom," after they discover new skills or interests, such as painting, gardening, playing group board games, and the like, or the joys of going out on field trips to such places as museums, theaters, zoos, and historical sites, and from using a range of previously unexperienced community amenities along with other seniors. Consequently, operators of adult day care programs should try to involve participants in such creative or experiential activities.

Adult day care programs also serve a crucial social function, easing the development of new friendships and aiding longtime companions to enjoy retirement activities together. Consequently, the individuals with a developmental disability may more readily adapt to the "care" nature of the setting and relish the opportunity to be helpful in a situation where they have usually been the object of help.

Many older persons with a developmental disability, while attending an adult day care program, also reside in a disability agency operated residence. Care should be taken to coordinate all aspects of the individual's program with the other agencies involved with the individual.

Commentary

This section offered some information on the nature of persons with a developmental disability and proposed that adult day care is a program model that will prove useful in meeting the long-term care needs of such individuals, particularly as they age.

The nature of the similarities to other adult day care users, in most instances, will overshadow any perceived differences that would set apart older persons with a developmental disability in adult day care settings. Care to the admission process, matching the needs of the individual to the general milieu offered by the adult day care site, and attention to the program and activities will lead to satisfaction on the part of the individuals and the staff with regard to the persons being served.

ACKNOWLEDGMENT: The material in this section was drawn from a number of sources, including *The Wit to Win: How to Integrate Older Persons with Developmental Disabilities into Community Aging Programs*, cited in the reading list.

READING LIST

Books on aging and disability

Hogg, James, Ph.D., S. Moss and D. Cooke, *Aging and Mental Handicap*. New York, N.Y.: Routledge, Chapman and Hall, Inc., 1988.

The authors present a review of aging and mental handicap literature from a British perspective. Chapters cover background issues, epidemiology, medical and psychiatric issues, intelligence and adaptive behavior, work and retirement, interventions for changing behavior, residential issues, and informal supports (411pp). It is available from Routledge Chapman and Hall, Inc. in the US (29 West 35th Street, New York, NY 10001).

Janicki, Matthew P., Ph.D. and H.M. Wisniewski, M.D., Ph.D., *Aging and Developmental Disabilities: Issues and Approaches*. Baltimore, Md.: Paul H. Brookes Publishing, 1985.

This extensive text, containing 26 chapters by various experts in the field, covers various aging and biological processes, legal and advocacy considerations, epidemiology, research and planning, service issues and practices, and residential and day programming, and family concerns (427pp). It is available from Paul H. Brookes Publishing (PO Box 10624, Baltimore, MD 21285; or call 800 638-3775).

Seltzer, Marsha M., Ph.D. and M. W. Krauss, Ph.D., *Aging and Mental Retardation: Extending the Continuum*. Washington, D.C.: American Association of Mental Retardation, 1987.

This American Association on Mental Retardation monograph includes a review of community and institutional-based day and residential programs currently in operation, and provides specific details of services models that appear to be particularly effective, as well as information on the role and structure of informal support networks (187pp). It is available from AAMR, 1719 Kalorama Road NW, Washington, DC 20009 (800-424-3688).

Stroud, Marion, E. Sutton and R. Roberts, Ph.D., *Expanding Options for Older Adults with Developmental Disabilities: A Practical Guide to Achieving Community Access*. Baltimore, Md.: Paul H. Brookes Publishing, 1988. This book is based upon the experiences of Dr. Roberts and her colleagues with Project ACCESS in Ohio (251pp). It contains background information on aging, the developmental disabilities, the needs of elderly persons with a disability, community organization, and treatment planning and implementation. A companion book, *Activities Handbook and Instructor's Guide*, is also available (255pp). The Handbook contains helpful information on specific program activities. Both are available from Paul H. Brookes Publishing (PO Box 10624, Baltimore, MD 21285; or call 800 638-3775).

Other Useful Publications

Ansello, Edward R., Ph.D. and A. Wells, Ph.D.,*Aging and Disabilities: The Intersection of Needs and Resources*. College Park, Md.: Center on Aging, University of Maryland, 1990.

Developed at the University of Maryland, this is a training manual for workers in aging and developmental disabilities agencies that covers a variety of topic areas useful in the implementation of integration efforts. Copies of the training manual are available from the Center on Aging, University of Maryland (College Park, MD 20742-2611; 301 454-5856).

Ansello, Edward F., Ph.D. and T. Rose, Ph.D., *Aging and Lifelong Disability: Partnership for the 21st Century*. College Park, Md.: Center on Aging, University of Maryland, 1989.

This is a summary of an invitational conference held at the Wingspread Conference Center in Racine, Wisconsin in June, 1987. Discussion summaries provide overviews of the relevant issues facing the states as they work toward integrating older Americans with developmental disabilities within mainstream aging network programs (82pp). It contains a series of recommendations for action and social policy to aid in effecting integration. It is available from the Virginia Commonwealth University's Center on Aging (Medical College of Virginia, Box 229, Richmond, VA 23298-0229).

LePore, Philip and M.P. Janicki, Ph.D. *The Wit to Win: How to Integrate Older Persons with Developmental Disabilities into Community Aging Programs*. Albany, N.Y.: New York State Office for the Aging, 1990.

A "How To Manual" designed to assist area agencies on aging and local mental retardation/developmental disabilities agencies on how to promote program integration in senior centers, congregate nutrition sites, and adult day care (96 pp). The manual, developed through funds provided by the state's developmental disabilities planning council, is based upon the experiences of a number of integration demonstration projects. Available from New York State Office for the Aging, Building 2, Empire State Plaza, Albany, NY 12223-0001 (call 518/486-2727).

New York State Office for the Aging. *Barriers and Strategies: Barriers to and Strategies for the Integration of Older Persons with Developmental Disabilities Within Aging Network Programs.* Albany, N.Y.: New York State Office for the Aging, 1987.

Developed and issued by the New York State Office for the Aging, this 36-page monograph outlines the preliminary aspects of the SOFA Community Integration Feasibility Project, identifying the problems localities may encounter as they implement integration projects of their own. The report outlines key actions at the state level and strategies to be employed at the local level to implement integration activities. Available from the State Office for the Aging, Building 2, Empire State Plaza, Albany, NY 12223-0001.

New York State Office of Mental Retardation and Developmental Disabilities, *New Directions for Seniors: Senior Day Program Demonstrations* and *New Directions for Seniors: Senior Day Program Expansion.* Albany, N.Y.: New York State Office of Mental Retardation and Developmental Disabilities, 1989, 1990.

Developed and issued by the New York State Office of Mental Retardation and Developmental Disabilities, these reports on adult day care type senior programs are available from the Bureau of Aging Services, NYS OMRDD, 44 Holland Avenue, Albany, NY 12229-0001.

Sailer, Margaret F. and S.J. Selkowitz, *Working with Developmentally Disabled Older Adults: A Training and Resource Manual.* Elwyn, Pa.: Elwyn Institutes, 1987.

A "how to" oriented manual on introducing and using a range of activities in programs specifically designed for older adults with developmental disabilities (73pp). Available from the Southeastern Pennsylvania Rehabilitation Center (SEPRC) of Elwyn Institutes, Baltimore Pike and Elwyn Road, Elwyn, PA 19063.

Thurman, Eunice. *All of Us: Strategies and Activity Ideas for Integrating Older Adults with Developmental Disabilities into Senior Centers.* Grand Rapids, Mich.: Kent Client Services, 1988.

This 109 page monograph covers a variety of activity suggestions for involving seniors in the day-to-day program of a senior center. The activities are presented within a means to evaluate the seniors potential for participation. This is available from Senior Center Integration Project, Kent Client Services, 1225 Lake Drive SE, Grand Rapids, MI 40506.

Videos

New York State Office of Mental Retardation and Developmental Disabilities, *Aging... A Shared Experience.* Albany, N.Y.: New York State Office of Mental Retardation and Developmental Disabilities, 1989.

This 20-minute video, developed and distributed by the New York State Office of Mental Retardation and Developmental Disabilities explores the twin themes of the effective community integration and friendships among older persons who are developmental disabled. It is equally appropriate for public education and staff training sessions. The videocassette (VHS format) is available from the Bureau of Aging Services, NYS OMRDD, 44 Holland Avenue, Albany, NY 12229-0001 (518 473-7855).

New York State Developmental Disabilities Planning Council, *Aging and Lifelong Disability (WT)*. New York, N.Y.: Hunter-Brookdale Center on Aging, 1990.

This 20-minute video, developed under a grant from the New York State Developmental Disabilities Planning Council, covers the physical and health aspects of aging among persons with developmental disabilities. Designed to be a training video, it provides useful information for families and program staff on similarities and dissimilarities related to the aging process among older persons with developmental disabilities. The video cassette (VHS format) is available from the Hunter-Brookdale Center on Aging, 425 East 25th Street, New York, NY 10010 (212 481-4426).

Profile of an Adult Day Health Center for Persons with Symptomatic HIV Infection

by Carol Kurland and Ellen Dryer

Introduction

New Jersey currently ranks fifth nationally in AIDS cases reported to the United States Centers for Disease Control (CDC). As of November 1, 1989 this number was 7,590, with an overall mortality of 62 percent. In New Jersey, 59 percent of AIDS cases are among intravenous drug abusers (IVDAs), while nationally intravenous drug abusers account for 28 percent of those infected. New Jersey also ranks third in the number of children with AIDS. The composition of the AIDS and AIDS-related

---

NOTE — Terms used include:

AIDS – acquired immunodeficiency syndrome, a clinical diagnosis based upon the presence of specific infections or malignancies.

ARC – AIDS-related complex, a specific group of chronic debilitating symptoms (including diarrhea, weight loss, fever) — not generally used at this time.

HIV – human immunodeficiency virus, the virus responsible for AIDS and HIV-related disorders.

HIV-related disorders – all health problems related to HIV infection.

Symptomatic HIV infection – HIV infection which is manifest in observable symptoms.

population in the state greatly influenced the development of resources to meet their care needs.

As the result of the tremendous demand for home and community-based care for the growing population, New Jersey in March 1987 responded with the creation of the nation's first specialized 2176 Medicaid Waiver program for persons with AIDS, AIDS Related Complex (ARC), and for children under 5 who are HIV positive. Along with start-up funds provided by the State Department of Health, Division on AIDS, this Medicaid Waiver served as the vehicle by which the first AIDS Adult Day Health Center was created and continues to be funded. Although adult day health care was available throughout the state as a regular Medicaid State Plan service, the Waiver enabled the reimbursement of an enhanced fee for services provided to this special population.

New Jersey's adult day health programs, regardless of the population served, must meet specific State Department of Health licensure requirements related to facility, staff, and program. Centers may be based in nursing homes, affiliated with hospitals, or exist as freestanding programs. Licensure requires a certificate of need and adherence to well-defined standards.

In the case of the adult day health center designed primarily for persons with AIDS/ARC, this facility operates as a freestanding center under the auspices of a church-run, drug-free treatment center, and is located in a downtown area of a North Jersey city. The center is situated on the first floor of a house renovated to accommodate both the adult day health center and a second floor AIDS residential unit.

Facility

An adult day health facility for persons with HIV disease must adhere to the same type of physical environment as any other facility serving a population with handicaps. It is recommended, however, that it not be isolated as an "AIDS" facility. Confidentiality is important to the clients and their families. It is easier for a person to attend a center called "Our House" or the "Grand Street Center" rather than "AIDS Day Care Center." Sensitivity to the social stigma of this disease is crucial. Vehicles used for transportation are also unmarked, since many clients may not have informed neighbors of their diagnosis.

The facility itself includes both indoor and outdoor space. The environment is secure and safe for both the participant, who may be visually impaired (CMW retinitis) or one suffering from AIDS dementia (encephalopathy). As people with AIDS live longer, they may become more functionally impaired. The majority of participants will develop some degree of AIDS dementia and have needs similar to those of persons with Alzheimer's disease, a condition that needs to be managed in a structured environment.

Infection control measures need to be integrated with sensitivity and diligence into the daily activities of the center. Guidelines from the Centers for Disease Control provide a basis for developing policies and procedures. Universal Precautions, defined by the Center for Disease Control, will provide a safe environment for all employees and clients. Universal Precautions are infection control guidelines based upon exposure to body fluids rather than the diagnosed disease state. Infection control policies need to be developed in the following areas: hand washing, gloves and protective garments, needle precautions, specimen handling, communicable diseases (such as tuberculosis and hepatitis), housekeeping, laundry, waste disposal, food service, and activities programming. State Health Departments usually have specific requirements for hazardous waste disposal in adult day health facilities. Client education for the home care of the person with HIV disease should be incorporated into the program. Many clients are concerned about transmitting the disease to their families and significant others. It has been helpful to provide written infection control guidelines for the client to take home and have available as a reference.

Staffing

Based upon the characteristics of the target population, the following staff positions are recommended in addition to essential care staff described in the standards:

● Certified Substance Abuse Counselor with experience in both individual and family counseling to provide on-site expertise in this area, particularly if the targeted population is, or has been, intravenous drug abusers.

● Psychiatric Consultant, due to the abundance of substance abusers who also have dual diagnoses of mental illness, as well as the increasing number of clients with AIDS dementia who may require psychiatric evaluation and intervention. Psychological support for staff is needed for their work with persons whose health deteriorates despite efforts to the contrary.

● Bereavement Consultant to assist the surviving

family members as well as to facilitate a staff support group. As evidenced by New Jersey's statistics, a high client mortality rate can be expected with this population; therefore, it is necessary to provide a mechanism for the staff to ventilate their feelings of loss and about death and dying. Families, including the surviving children, require special support and bereavement counseling, as their usual sources of community support such as clergy, neighbors, and friends may not be available to them because of the social stigma of the disease.

All staff should have experience and be comfortable working with the population served: inner city, low-income, homosexual, substance abusers, and persons with AIDS.

● Volunteers, such as a local "Buddies" group, may serve as a supplemental resource to the center providing in-home assistance. Many other opportunities exist for volunteers to become involved. This involvement greatly enriches the quality of the program while building a valuable, much needed link to the community and fostering greater understanding of the disease.

Population

For the most part, the target population is adults with physical, psycho-social and/or mental impairment who require assistance and supervision (Category A). However, occasionally the center will be utilized as a transition facility for those adults who need restorative or rehabilitative services in order to achieve their optimal level of functioning (Category B), such as someone nearly blind from CMV retinitis or a client who suffers from acute depression after being diagnosed with an opportunistic infection (such as Kaposi's Sarcoma or Pneumocytis Pneumonia).

An adult day center serving persons with AIDS must provide a warm and accepting environment. This emotional support, along with strong medical supervision, allows clients to remain at home in an improved state of wellness. Without the adult day health center, suffering from isolation and stigma leads to loneliness and despair.

From our experience, individuals served by the center are of diverse ages (19-69), but are primarily in the 25-40 age range. In accordance with New Jersey's risk groups, 63 percent of the population are IVDAs. The remaining persons are a mixture of other risk groups, homosexual, bisexual, and heterosexual population. They are usually single (never married, widowed, or divorced) and rarely currently married. More than half of the persons served are Black and over 60 percent are males. The largest number (over 50 percent) live with parents or adult children and, subsequently, the primary caregivers are parents. Individuals enroll in the center because of their chronic physical health problems, social isolation, deterioration of medical status, increased dependency in ADLs and IADLs, psychiatric problems, and because the primary caregiver needs relief.

Services

In addition to the essential services described in the standards, the following services are appropriate to this specialized center.

Nursing

Active treatment is provided: for example, prophylactic breathing treatments to prevent Pneumocytis Pneumonia, central line medication administration, or dressing changes. Many clients live alone or with dysfunctional family units. Visiting nurse agencies are shortstaffed and may not serve all inner city areas, where many clients reside; therefore, clients may not have access to these needed nursing services through traditional methods. The adult day health center becomes the primary site for nursing supervision and direct care. HIV disease is progressive and relentless in nature. Its progression is not on a straight downward curve but rather on a roller coaster. Some clients may appear to be near death and yet recover; others may seem perfectly well one day and then be hospitalized the next. The nursing staff requires a special level of expertise in assessing the medical and health care status and daily needs of HIV clients.

The medication utilized in HIV care may be new or experimental; therefore, facilities need to develop policies and procedures in regard to the use of experimental or investigational drugs.

Education

HIV care is client-centered care. The adult day health center should include a strong educational component with a goal towards client empowerment. Issues to be addressed include:

- prevention of HIV disease
- transmission of HIV disease
- safe sex guidelines
- guidelines for home care

● signs and symptoms of opportunistic infections

● medication regimens (experimental treatment issues)

● drug treatment

● methadone maintenance

● pain management

● psychosocial concerns

● death and dying.

Drug Treatment

Service linkages need to be established with outpatient and residential drug treatment centers as well as methadone programs to facilitate client referrals. Community groups such as Narcotics Anonymous and Alcoholics Anonymous may be invited to hold group meetings within the facility when appropriate.

Insofar as many persons with AIDS are chronic substance abusers, it is desirable to institute a drug policy that aggressively prohibits the use of drugs by clients while they are en route to the center or in attendance. Since clients cannot realistically be expected to abstain totally from the use of illegal substances, the effects of these drugs must be a consideration within the overall treatment program. Repeated violations of the substance abuse policy could result in exclusion from the center.

Child Care

More and more women of child-bearing age are infected with the HIV virus. Minimally, linkages with child care service need to be developed so that clients with small children can attend the center.

Activities in the AIDS Center

Participants present a wide range as well as varied life styles and experiences. The recreation program, therefore, must provide a diverse and flexible schedule based upon the individual needs of the participants. For example, participants with a substance abuse history beginning as teenagers may never have developed hobbies or interests outside of compulsive drug-seeking behavior. Whereas, other participants may have a long work history or have been housewives with many social activities and interests.

Individual recreational assessments, required on all participants, are integrated into a interdisciplinary care plan that includes input from the nursing, social work, dietary, and medical staff.

Dual activity programming is also a consideration due to the diversity of participants' needs. For example, an array of arts and crafts projects may be scheduled at the same time as card games, chess, and checkers, rather than one specific arts and crafts project. Needless to say, this increases the workload of activity staff and requires the cooperation of staff from other disciplines (nursing, social work) to supervise and participate in the activity program.

Daily activities at the center include discussions about health and social issues, relaxation therapy, arts and crafts, risk reduction/substance abuse programs, day trips to local parks, bowling, games, and guest speakers. Participants enjoy involvement in community activities; for example, making Christmas gifts for children who reside in an AIDS group foster care home.

Support Groups

Due to the social stigma surrounding HIV disease, support groups have become an important part of the activities program. Many participants do not have supportive families and many have lost their friends either to HIV disease or because of their fear of the illness. Groups with varying foci are scheduled every morning for one hour. A weekly group sampling may be as follows: Pastoral Care (spiritual support facilitated by clergy), high risk reduction (facilitated by Narcotics Anonymous), meditation and guided imagery, peer support, and an educational support group to which community speakers are invited. This may include nutritionists, funeral directors, and lawyers.

Memorial Services and Bereavement

Inevitably, members of the center will die of complications of HIV disease. Death has become an important issue in adapting to a chronic illness role. Participants express many fears about death and dying; they may be grieving simultaneously for the loss of their friends and for the internal loss of their own hopes and dreams. Staff must also confront fears and beliefs regarding their own mortality as they witness so many people of the same age dying.

Memorial services conducted by local clergy are held at the center whenever a participant dies; the family of the deceased member is invited to participate. A special candle is lit during this service and all participants and staff participate in remembering the deceased member. Wakes and funerals are also attended by both staff and participants together as a group.

General Information For All Adult Day Care Centers

Universal Precautions are recommended in all health care settings, since it is impossible to know who may or may not be infected with HIV. Many clinicians may not think of AIDS as a diagnosis for the older person as readily as they would for a younger person with the same symptoms (Weiler, 1989). In the United States 10 percent of the patients with AIDS were over 50, 2.5 percent over 60, and 0.4 percent over 70 (Hargreaves, et al, 1988).

Complex Morbidity and Increased Mortality
HIV is a complex disease with numerous manifestations whereby the client's condition and functional capacity may change on a daily basis. The disease takes a "roller coaster" type course rather than a slow and steady decline. As a result, staff may require increased and ongoing medical findings.
On, average there may be more terminal care in the HIV clientele than normally encountered with the elderly (Benjamin, 1989).

Staff Education
Prior to admitting any HIV participant all staff should be educated regarding Universal Precautions, HIV transmission, confidentiality, and employee work policies regarding accidental exposure to HIV.

Public Relations

Once the staff is educated, other clients and their families need orientation to HIV disease as well as a forum to ask questions and ventilate fears.

Conclusion

Many persons who are HIV-seropositive are currently residing at home, but are isolated in many ways, cut off from social interaction and from the support services necessary for their continued existence outside a hospital or nursing home setting. Aside from the cost-effectiveness of treating these individuals on an out-patient basis, it is neither appropriate nor humane to force institutionalization for individuals who want to remain home. Adult day care for HIV-seropositive persons provides most of the medical and health support services needed, as well as opportunities for socialization, peer contact, and respite for caregivers.

References

Benjamin, A.E., "Chronic Care: Perspectives on AIDS and Aging" *Generations*. Fall 1989, pages 19-22.

Benjamin, A.E., "Nursing Home Care for Persons with HIV Illnesses," *Generations*. Fall 1989, pages 63-64.

Bressler, Jeanette, AIDS and Aging: A Report to the Philadelphia Commission on AIDS. Philadelphia, Pa.: unpublished, August 1988.

Catalano, Donald J., "What is the Impact of AIDS on Senior Services?" *Aging Connection* 8(2). April/May 1987, page 10.

Catalano, Donald J., "Adapting Community Based Senior Services to Serve People with AIDS/ARC," Proceedings of the 41st Annual Meeting of the Gerontological Society of America, San Francisco. Washington, D.C.: Gerontological Society of American, 1988.

Centers for Disease Control. Recommendations for Prevention of HIV Transmission in Health Care Settings. *Morbidity and Mortality Weekly Report,* 1987; 36: (Suppl. No 2S).

Centers for Disease Control. Update: Universal Precautions for Prevention of Transmission of Human Immunodeficiency Virus, Hepatitis B Virus, and Other Bloodborne Pathogens in Health Care Settings. *Morbidity and Mortality Weekly Report*, 1988; 37: 229-234.

Centers for Disease Control. Update: Acquired Immunodeficiency Syndrome - US, 1981-1988. *Morbidity and Mortality Weekly Report*, 1989: 38; 229-236.

Eisdorfer, Carl, "AIDS, Alzheimer's and Aging: What are the Connections?" *Aging Connection* 9(5). October/November 1988, page 7.

Hargreaves, M.R., G.N. Fuller, and B. Gazzard, "Occult AIDS: Pneumocystis Carinii Pneumonia in Elderly People," *The British Medical Journal.* 1988, 297 (6650): 721-22.

Hughes, A.M., J.P. Martin, and P. Frank, *AIDS Home Care and Hospice Manual.* San Francisco: AIDS Home and Hospice Program, VNA of San Francisco, 1987.

Kaplan, M., "HIV Infection: An Emerging Problem in Elderly Patients," Proceedings of the 40th Annual Meeting of the Gerontological Society of America, Washington, D.C. Washington, D.C.: Gerontological Society of America, 1987.

Koop, C. Everett, Surgeon General's Report on Acquired Immune Deficiency Syndrome. Washington, D.C.: U.S. Public Health Service, 1986.

Lynette, Eileen and D. Catalano, "Can Programs for Frail Elders Also Serve AIDS Patients?" *Aging Connection* 9(5). October/November 1988.

Lynn, Joanne, "The Impact of AIDS on the Care of Older Persons," Proceedings of the 41st Annual Meeting of the Gerontological Society of American, San Francisco. Washington, D.C.: Gerontological Society of America, 1988.

McNally, Len, J. Oppenheimer and A. Seiman, " Development of a Continuum of Long-Term Care Services for People with AIDS," Proceedings of the 41st Annual Meeting of the Gerontological Society of America, San Francisco. Washington, D.C.: Gerontological Society of America, 1988.

Sabin, T.D., "AIDS: The New `Great Imitator'," *Journal of the American Geriatrics Society* 35, 1987, pages 467-471.

Weiler, Philip G., D. Mungas, and S. Pomerantz, "AIDS as a Cause of Dementia in the Elderly," *Journal of the American Geriatrics Society* 36. Fall 1989, pages 139-41.

Weiler, Philip G., 1989 "AIDS and Dementia." *Generations.* Fall 1989, pages 16-18.

Recommendations for Adult Day Care Centers Serving Individuals with Visual Impairments, Hearing Loss, and Communication Disorders

by Arlene Snyder

Introduction

As many as 86 percent of persons over 65 have one or more chronic conditions that have a potential effect on communication. It is this older, frail group with multiple handicapping conditions who are likely to need adult day care services. Blindness/visual impairments, hearing loss, and communication disorders are common problems experienced by adult day care participants. Adult day care programs must address the specialized needs of individuals with these impairments.

A successful adult day care program serving persons with sensory impairments/ communication disorders is characterized by:

- ● staff trained in effective ways of communicating

- ● a safe and supportive environment

● a program of therapeutic activities that promotes the participant's dignity and self-esteem and independent functioning

● educational and supportive services to family/ caregivers, designed to strengthen their caregiving abilities and coping skills, and assist them with identifying and utilizing community resources

● relationships with organizations and professionals trained to work with older people who have vision loss, hearing impairments, and communication disorders.

Sensory Impairments/ Communication Disorders

As many as 70 percent of older adults have a problem with communication. Our communication system, which involves speaking, hearing, and understanding the speech of others, plays a vital role in all aspects of every day life. When communication processes are damaged by disorders of speech, language, or hearing, the effects are always serious. The number of older adults with communication problems is expected to grow as the number of older adults increases, and as more people survive illnesses and accidents that result in speech, language, or hearing disorders.

Disorders of communication that affect older people may result from hearing impairment, stroke, cancer, or other diseases of the larynx, Parkinsonism, or other neurological disorders. Communication disorders include difficulty with speaking and with understanding verbal messages.

The communication disorders that most frequently affect older people include:

Aphasia (Disorder of language)

Aphasia may result in a reduced ability to understand what others are saying, to express oneself, or to be understood. The ability to understand oral directions, to read, to write, and to deal with numbers may also be disturbed. Strokes are the major cause of aphasia in the older population.

Dysarthria (Disorder of speech)

Dysarthria interferes with normal control of the speech mechanism. Speech may be slurred or otherwise difficult to understand. Diseases such as Parkinson's Disease, Multiple Sclerosis, strokes, and accidents can cause dysarthria.

Hearing Impairment

The term *hearing impairment* refers to any degree of loss of hearing of loudness or pitch that is outside the range for normal. The term *deaf* refers to those hearing impairments of a profound degree.

Presbycusis is the loss of auditory sensitivity that occurs as a part of aging. With varying degrees of severity, Presbycusis affects approximately 60 percent of individuals over 65 years of age in the United States. Presbycusis is permanent because nerve cells have degenerated. Presbycusis is more common and more severe for men, and it gradually worsens with age. Many of those with presbycusis describe the problem as being able to "hear" what others are saying, but being unable to understand what is being said. The resulting difficulty in communicating may make the individual appear confused or forgetful.

An unfortunate consequence of a hearing impairment is a feeling of isolation that results when communication deteriorates. Hearing loss often leads to withdrawal and poor self-image. For older people who live with families, hearing loss can create tension in the family.

Providing effective communication with others is the key to keeping individuals with hearing impairments from living in isolation.

Other Communication Problems

Brain diseases such as Alzheimer's disease that result in progressive loss of mental faculties may affect memory; orientation to time, place, and people; and organization of thought processes—all of which may result in reduced ability to communicate.

Visual Impairments

The National Center for Health Statistics reports that 70 percent of the 1.4 million persons with severe visual impairments are over the age of 65. According to a study conducted by the National Society for the Prevention of Blindness, a majority of those over the age of 75 years are likely to experience some visual handicaps that may affect their abilities to perform the necessary activities of daily living. Low vision aids and rehabilitative services can help prevent such limitations and enhance functional vision.

The prevalence of multiple impairments involving vision also increases with age. Blindness and severe visual impairment are conditions whose handicapping effects vary with the individual, depending on the degree of remaining useful sight, the person's ability to use residual sight effectively and efficiently, the presence of other impairments, and age. Vision loss can have a profound effect on the quality of life of many elderly persons. Visual impairments can affect communications skills, mobility, and daily living skills. Vision loss may be met with depression, loneliness, fear, anxiety, anger, and helplessness. The trauma of vision loss compounds the emotional difficulties of dealing with the changes with age.

It is important to note also that in all adult day care centers it is necessary to respond to the vision losses or changes that accompany aging for most older persons. Although not considered impairments, the following changes must be accommodated:

● increased sensitivity to glare

● need for additional light

● decreased contrast-sensitivity

● decreased color sense

● slower adaptation to different lighting levels.

Appropriate and responsive accommodations are listed in the following recommendations–particularly those included in the Facility section.

The Standards

Administration and Organization

In addition to the requirements for administration and organization in the overall standards, the adult day care center serving these participants should:

● institute organizational policies that respond to the needs of individuals with sensory impairments/ communication disorders

● develop a plan to provide ongoing health prevention and screening programs for participants in adult day care

● develop a plan for education and support of families/ caregivers to help identify problems, strengthen caregiving abilities and coping skills.

Services: Individual Plan of Care

The development of the individual plan of care should proceed as indicated in the overall standards with some additional provisions. During intake, special attention must be paid to assessing functional ability.

The development of the plan of care should include the following:

● the family/caregiver should be involved in all phases of the individual plan of care including admission, short and long-term goals, and discharge

● an assessment that includes an evaluation by a trained professional of an individual's visual impairment, hearing impairment, and/or communication problems to include the nature of the loss, date of onset, degree of impairment, how the impairment affects communication, effect on general function, impact/level of adjustment, compensatory behaviors, use of assistive devices, other medical conditions, pre-morbid level of function (personal, social, intellectual, vocational), and the current status of the condition causing the impairment

● an assessment of social supports and of services available for the participant and the family/caregiver

● an assessment of the individual's interests before his or her impairment, so adaption can be made to enable the person to continue to participate (for example, large-print books, self-threading needles, talking books)

● ongoing monitoring of health to include annual physical examinations and regular health screening/ prevention programs, especially vision and hearing screening programs

● recommendations for the use of assistive devices and educational counseling on their use, for participants and their families/caregivers.

Essential and Specialized Services

All of the required services described in the overall standards are necessary. Education services for the participant and family/caregiver should be a strong component.

Services should also include access and referral to other rehabilitation services, support groups for caregivers, support groups for participants, and appropriate medical services. Also recommended:

● use of consultants who could work with and advise the staff, coordinate and conduct staff training, provide ongoing consultation to staff, and assess, develop, and evaluate the treatment program for individuals;

● access to a rehabilitation counselor to provide counseling to individuals on disability-related issues and to coordinate the special services or therapies from other agencies;

● access to an orientation and mobility instructor to provide the participant who is blind or visually impaired with mobility instruction and orientation to the adult day care site and to facilitate the overall rehabilitation process;

● access to an audiologist who could identify and evaluate impaired hearing, determine the need for hearing rehabilitation, and establish an individualized program to help participants make the best use of their hearing;

● access to a speech-language pathologist to evaluate and diagnose speech and language disorders and to design and implement a treatment program;

● arrangements with agencies serving those who are blind or visually impaired, those who are deaf or hearing impaired and individuals with communication disorders for consultation, training, and assistance as needed; (Staff of both programs should work together to plan programs, to educate the staff, and to provide services to participants in need.)

● arrangements for low vision demonstration, for participants with visual impairments, that would include adaptive devices, such as signature guides and magnifying glasses.

Therapeutic Activities

The therapeutic activity plan is an integral part of the overall plan of care.

Activities and services should be designed to enhance the individual's ability to communicate. The activities schedule must take into account the special needs of individuals with sensory impairments. Activities that focus on the different senses and provide multiple forms of communication and expression are needed.

In addition to the overall standards for therapeutic activities, there should be a comprehensive range of activities that:

- provides peer counselors to offer support and enable the participant to be active and involved

- provides a wide range of activities that stimulates the senses

- provides language-based activities and games for those with hearing impairment

- enables the participants to maintain/develop their maximum level of functioning

- promotes feelings of self-confidence and self-worth to counteract any lack of motivation and feelings of helplessness that often accompany the loss of vision/hearing/communication skills.

Staffing

It is essential that staff members have knowledge of hearing and vision loss and speech/language disorders, any concomitant communication problems, and group process skills. Staff should be receptive and trained to work with individuals with sensory impairments/communication disorders.

In addition to the staffing requirements stated in the overall standards, the adult day care center should do the following:

● Provide orientation and in-service training for the staff on sensory impairments/communication disorders, sensitivity training, avoidance of over-protection, an emphasis on promoting independent functioning, terminology, and the impact of sensory impairments/communication disorders on dementing illnesses.

● Provide training for staff on mobility instruction techniques, use of adaptive devices, and communication skills.

Facility

The physical facility and operation should protect the participant from injury and enhance the ability to function independently. The facility should provide the equipment necessary to accommodate the special needs of those with sensory impairment. An orientation and mobility instructor should assess the adult day care site to point out obstacles and make suggestions for adaption. Sound and visual systems suitable to effective communication should be provided.

In addition to the facility requirements of the overall standards, the facility should do the following:

● Use sheer curtains and venetian blinds which reduce glare but still allow the participants to see outside.

● Employ the use of cues so that physical factors will enhance and support functioning.

● Provide adequate levels of illumination to enable individuals with visual impairment to read lips. Provide focused light at work surfaces.

● Use non-glare floor and furniture finishes that do not reflect light. Low-gloss finishes and paints, and textured fabrics, help to reduce glare. Florescent lights are hard on older eyes.

● Use incandescent lighting or frosted bulbs to reduce glare. Provide lighting that is consistent from room to room.

● Use furnishings and equipment that are safe, comfortable, and appropriate for use by individuals with sensory impairments/other disabilities.

● Provide raised letters and numbers on doors and elevators and hardened fluorescent highlighting to provide tactile clues.

● Provide an environment that is clutter-free. Furnishings should be strategically placed to reduce the likelihood of falls and collisions. The design should facilitate the individuals' movement through the center and involvement in activities.

● Provide acoustical control to decrease noise and increase amplification. Use sound systems that can be adjusted to accommodate hearing loss.

● Provide specialized alarm systems.

● Use handrails.

● Use bright, contrasting colors (doorways from walls, chair seat from floor, dishes from the table cover).

● Use extra-large print on signs, clocks, and schedules.

● Provide assistive listening devices (ALDs). ALDs are designed to assist the hearing-impaired individual to function more efficiently. ALDs include both amplifying sound systems and alerting devices.

● Provide talking tapes and large print newsletters that report on daily/weekly activities and events.

● Provide decoders for television, so captioned programs can be made available.

● Use large print and items that are extra large.

● For significant hearing loss, audioloops and other amplification systems should be utilized.

● Use visual aids, signs, and flashing lights to enhance communication access for deaf people.

● Provide low-vision aids, such as magnifying lenses.

● Provide communication boards for individuals with aphasia.

Evaluation

In addition to the evaluation components of the overall standards, the following information should be solicited:

● Input should be obtained from consultants on the participants' needs/progress.

● Input should be obtained from the participant and family/caregiver on their satisfaction with the program, on the quality of care provided, and on any unmet needs.

References

American Speech - Language Hearing Association, *Management of Hearing Impairment in Older Adults*. Rockville, Md.: American Speech - Language Hearing Association, 1984.

Gritz, Janet M., "Communication Disorders and Aging," *Aging Network News*. 1985.

Horowitz, Amy and L. Cassels, *Vision Education and Outreach: Identifying and Serving Visually Impaired Elderly*. New York, N.Y.: New York Association for the Blind, 1985.

Hull, Raymond H. and K.M. Griffin, *Communication Disorders in Aging*. Newburg Park, Calif: Sage Publication, Inc., 1989.

Laufer, M. Barbara, *Have You Heard? Hearing Loss and Aging*. Washington, D.C.: American Association of Retired Persons, 1984.

Luey, H.S., *An Unobscured View: Meeting the Service Needs of Hearing Impaired Seniors*. Washington, D.C.: The National Academy, Gallaudet University, 1987.

National Society for the Prevention of Blindness, *Vision Problems in the U.S.* New York, N.Y.: National Society for the Prevention of Blindness, 1980.

Oberstar, Jo, *White House Conference on Aging. Report on Elderly Hearing Impaired People*. Bethesda, Md.: Self Help for Hard of Hearing People, 1981.

Snyder, Arlene A., H.J. Dom, D.E. Biegel, and B. Beisgen, *Service Coordination for the Blind and Visually Impaired Elderly*. Harrisburg, Pa.: Pennsylvania Department of Aging, 1986.

U.S. Congress, House, *Blindness and the Elderly*. Hearing before the Select Committee on Aging, U.S. House of Representatives, Ninety-ninth Congress, First Session, 1985. Publication No. 99-519.

U.S. Congress, Office of Technology Assessment, *Hearing Impairment and Elderly People: A Background Paper*. Washington, D.C.: Government Printing Office. Pub.No. (OTA-BP-BA-30), 1986.

U.S. Congress, Senate, Special Committee on Aging, *Vision Impairment Among Older Americans*, Hearing before the U.S. Senate, 95th Congress, Session, 1978.

Resources

Abramson, Marcia and P. Lovas, Editors, *Aging and Sensory Change: An Annotated Bibliography.* Washington, D.C.: The Gerontological Society of America, 1988.

Alexander Graham Bell Association for the Deaf, 2417 Volta Place, NW, Washington, DC 20007.

American Foundation for the Blind, 15 West 16th Street, New York, NY 10011.

American Speech - Language, Hearing Association, 10801 Rockville Pike, Rockville, MD 20852.

National Aphasia Association, c/o New York University Medical Center, 400 East 34th Street, New York, NY 10016.

National Association of the Deaf, 814 Thayer Avenue, Silver Spring, MD 20910.

National Institute on Deafness and Other Communication Disorders, National Institutes of Health, Building 31, Room 1B-62, Bethesda, MD 20892.

New York Association for the Blind, National Center for Vision and Aging, 3620 Northern Boulevard, Long Island City, NY 11101.

Sensory Technology Information Service, National Clearinghouse on Technology and Aging, University Center on Aging, University of Massachusetts Medical Center, 55 Lake Avenue North, Worcester, Massachusetts 01655.

Noted Resource For Adult Day Care and Visual Impairments:
Individuals interested in additional references on services to those with visual impairments as well as the adaptation of adult day care programs to meet the needs of this special population may contact:

Joan Joseph, Assistant Vice President
Adult Day Services
The Jewish Guild for the Blind
15 West 65th Street
New York, NY 10023
(212) 769-6351.

Adult Day Care for Those with Mental Health Needs

by Linda Van Buskirk

Three characteristics distinguish an adult day care program that serves individuals who have mental health problems.

First is the dominance of psyco-therapeutic modes of intervention. This intervention includes verbal, as well as drug, therapy. These therapies are provided by qualified professional staff in individual and/or small group settings. Serving this population of individuals also means that the adult day care staff must be able to respond to acute psychotic behavior and suicidal threats. Crisis intervention procedures are essential, as is psychiatric consultation.

The second distinguishing characteristic is the necessity of dealing with behavior created by institutionalization and/or the effects of long term drug therapy. Typical behaviors exhibited by adult day care members include, for example, an inability to make decisions, excessive smoking and intake of coffee, the need to be in a very structured environment, the inability to tolerate stimulation (such as an unknown person entering the room), and passivity and attention-getting behaviors (the inability to express feelings appropriately). Those suffering from the long-term effects of drug therapy can also have dryness of mouth, lip smacking, chin wagging, blurred vision, confusion and involuntary twitches. These behaviors may give the day care member a "different" appearance. In some settings, this could cause others to respond with fear and rejection.

The significant strain on family relationships and/or the lack of family involvement is the third characteristic. Psychotic behaviors, chronic mental health problems, and repeated or lengthy institutionalizations frequently result in strained family relationships—even in the termination of family relationship. Ideally, staff in a center serving this population should be skilled in using family therapy techniques.

The presence of these characteristics creates special challenges for the center staff and may add to services and staffing considerations. Serving individuals with mental health problems means that adult day care staff must be able to respond to institutionalized behavior, acute psychotic behavior, and suicidal threats. A mental health day program must comply with state regulations that will govern staffing and appropriate training. In a non-mental health setting, psychiatric consultation, often related to medication issues, and professional social work services are necessary. The latter will include interventions, on-going evaluation of needed services, assessment of progress, individual therapy, and crisis intervention.

Written procedures and agreements concerning referrals and discharge, crisis intervention, involuntary hospitalizations, and followup care are essential. Most mental health agencies communicate regularly with other identified mental health agencies. It is very important that the day care facility become part of this network.

Small group activities that can be therapeutic in nature can also require a wide range of professional skill. These activities may include discussion groups, cooking classes, music groups, even a writing group. In attempting to deal with behaviors created by institutionalization or by mental illness, certain activities are helpful in the areas of appropriate expression of feeling and decisionmaking. These are two important areas in which the participant is likely to need assistance and direction.

For example, a small group activity that fosters the expression of feelings might be called "Self Disclosures." Topics for discussion in the group can include the following:

- how do I feel when I am treated like a sick person?
- how can I be assertive in relationships with my family and friends?
- how do I ask for help when I need it? and
- why do I have to wait my turn to talk in a group?

An example of an activity that strengthens decisionmaking skills for a person who is depressed could be a cooking group. In such a group an individual is asked to:

- plan a meal
- develop a budget
- shop
- prepare the meal, serve it, and eat it.

A very basic group for dealing with behaviors created by institutionalization could be called the "Me" group. This type of group would assist people to learn to wait their turn in line or when speaking, relearn appropriate eating habits, and re-establish a concern for clothing and dressing. It can re-educate the participants in skills needed in the community. For example, structuring a trip to a store to purchase an item in order to allow the participant to carry out the entire transaction is important.

It is also important to provide an environment and facility that minimize distractions. Loud noises, the movement of other people into and out of the program area, and other activities in the same area can be distracting. Small group activities are best conducted in well-ventilated, well-lit rooms that have comfortable furniture. Private interviewing areas are not only important for confidentiality, but can be used to help calm someone who has become anxious.

The issues raised by the lack of adequate family involvement often have a direct impact on staff. The most significant problem is excessive staff involvement in the participant's life. This situation tends to increase the participant's dependency problems, and it hampers his or her ability to develop other informal supports. Termination problems develop for participants when staff members leave the agency. This can have a severe impact upon the participant who has come to trust and depend upon the staff person beyond the normal client/professional relationship. The boundaries become confused and the participant may feel rejected by losing a significant support person. As staff become too involved in participants' lives, they risk burn-out, feelings of guilt, loss of professional objectivity, and increased anger toward absent, or less involved, family members.

In order to avoid this problem it is essential that the staff believe that family relationships can be repaired and work toward that goal, although the amount of involvement will vary from family to family. Techniques available to the staff include the involvement of the participant and family in case conferences and in non-threatening social activities, as well as family treatment.

Finally, the question of integrating participants with

mental illness into the general population is a very difficult one to address. Ideally, this should be a goal for individuals. The key to successful integration is appropriate behavior and expectations on everyone's part. Staff must be realistic, and all people must prepare. Roleplaying, discussions, and education must be used with both the mental health and non-mental health populations.

Resource

Monk, Abraham, D.S.W., *The Integration of Frail Elderly into Senior Centers*, New York, N.Y.: Brookdale Institute on Aging and Adult Human Development, Columbia University, January 1988.

A study completed in 1987, *The Integration of Frail Elderly into Senior Centers*, highlights some problems that may also face adult day care programs. This study found that behavioral and emotional problems were perceived as the most difficult to handle in ongoing programs. Sensorial, memory, and mobility problems were easier to deal with and accept. This study concluded that the discussion of issues and education of members was critical to success.

National Institute on Adult Daycare

Delegate Council
1988-1990

CHAIR
Ruth Von Behren, Ph.D.
Day Health Care Specialist
On Lok Senior Health Services
San Francisco, Calif.

CHAIR-ELECT
Mary Ann Outwater
Executive Director
New Horizons at Choate
Woburn, Mass.

SECRETARY
Kathryn S. Katz
Regional Director
Connecticut Community
Care, Inc.
New Haven, Conn.

IMMEDIATE PAST CHAIR
Kay Larmer
Coordinator, Adult Day
Health Care
Fairfax County Health
Fairfax, Va.

AT-LARGE DELEGATES

Dorothy Ohnsorg
Adult Day Health Care
Coordinator
V.A. Medical Center
Minneapolis, Minn.

Bonnie Walson
Director
Heritage Day Health
Columbus, Ohio

REGIONAL DELEGATES

Region I
Carole J. Barnard
Executive Director
Elder House Adult Day Care
Norwalk, Conn.

Region II
Paulette Zigelstein
Director, Day Services
Jewish Home of Rochester
Rochester, N.Y.

Region III
Phyllis Conrad
Director
Elder Day Centre
Chambersburg, Pa.

Region IV
Thelma D. Freeze
Executive Director
L.I.F.E. Center, Inc.
Concord, N.C.

Region V
Susan Ganote
Day Care Services
Oakwood Hospital Corp.
Dearborn, Mich.

Region VI
Barbara C'DeBaca, Manager
Frail Elderly Programs
Albuquerque, N.M.

Region VII
Sister John Antonio Miller,
C.PP.S
St. Elizabeth Adult Day Care
St. Louis, Mo.

Region VIII
Jody Mayer
Director
Homestead Adult Day Program
Longmont United Hospital
Longmont, Colo.

Region IX
Eileen Lynette
Director, Long Term Care
John Muir Medical Center
Walnut Creek, Calif.

Region X
Betty Sanders
Director
Seattle Day Care Center
for Adults
Seattle, Wash.

NIAD Task Force on Standards
1988 - 1990

CHAIR
Mary Ann Outwater
Executive Director
New Horizons at Choate
Woburn, Mass.

MEMBERS

Linda Crossman
Executive Director
Marin Adult Day Health Services
San Anselmo, Calf.

Marvin Kaiser, Ph.D.
Acting Associate Dean, College
of Arts and Sciences
Kansas State University
Manhattan, Kan.

Hazel Croy
Adult Day Health Program
Manager
Massachusetts Department of
Public Welfare
Boston, Mass.

Kathryn S. Katz
Regional Director
Connecticut Community Care, Inc.
New Haven, Conn.

Eleanor Davis
President
Pennsylvania Medical Society
Auxiliary
Pittsburgh, Pa.

Winnifred Kelly
Director
Project L.I.N.C.
Pompton Lakes, N.J.

Carolyn French
Consultant
Alzheimer's Program
Atlanta, Ga.

Suzi Kennedy
Director
Life Enrichment Center
Shelby, N.C.

Carol H. Kurland
Administrator
Office of Home Care Programs
Department of Human Services
Division of Medical Assistance
and Health Services
Trenton, N.J.

Carrie Sinkler-Parker
State Health and Human Services
Financing Commission
Columbia, S.C.

Kay Larmer
Coordinator
Adult Day Health Care
Fairfax County Health Dept.
Fairfax, Va.

Arlene Snyder
Executive Director
Vintage, Inc.
Pittsburgh, Pa.

Eileen Lynette
Director, Long Term Care
John Muir Medical Center
Walnut Creek, Calf.

Ruth Von Behren, Ph.D.
Adult Day Health Care Specialist
On Lok Senior Health Services
San Francisco, Calf.

Paul Maginn
Director
McAuley Bergan Center
Omaha, Neb.

Jane C. Wessely
Coordinator
Department of Health and Mental
Hygiene
Health Systems Financing
Baltimore, Md.

Dorothy W. Ohnsorg
Coordinator
Adult Day Health Care
V.A. Medical Center
Minneapolis, Minn.

Margaret Williams
Vice President
Bethany Center
Horseheads, N.Y.

Betty Sanders
Director
Seattle Day Center for Adults
Seattle, Wash.

Paulette Zigelstein
Director
Day Services
Jewish Home of Rochester
Rochester, N.Y.

Special Subcommittee on Guidelines for Programs Serving Individuals with Alzheimer's Disease and Other Dementias

Carolyn French
Consultant
Alzheimer's Program
Atlanta, Ga.

Kay Larmer
Coordinator, Adult Day Health Care
Fairfax County Health Dept.
Fairfax, Va.

Suzi Kennedy
Director
Life Enrichment Center
Shelby, N.C.

Paulette Zigelstein
Director, Day Services
Jewish Home of Rochester
Rochester, N.Y.

Resources

General Resources Useful in Developing any Adult Day Care Program

Goldston, Sudie Maready, *Adult Day Care: A Basic Guide*. Owings Mills, Md.: National Health Publishing, 1989.

An introductory guide to starting an adult day care center, this comprehensive resource provides a practical approach to aid in design, implementation, and execution of an adult day care program, including step-by-step guides for all phases of program management (360 pages). It is available from National Health Publishing for $40—for address, see Sources, below.

Planning and Managing Adult Day Care: Pathways to Success. Linda Cook Webb, M.S.G., ed., Owings Mills, Md.: National Health Publishing, 1988.

Written by the editor along with 10 contributors, this is a useful reference for developing and improving adult day care programs. Topics include planning, services, financial management, record-keeping, computers, evaluation, and research (350 pages). It is available from National Health Publishing for $36—for address, see Sources, below.

Resources That Focus on Alzheimer's Disease and Other Dementias

American Association of Homes for the Aging, *Guide to Caring for Mentally Impaired Elderly*. Washington, D.C.: American Association of Homes for the Aging, 1985.

This is a guide for residential facilities with much to offer the adult day care center, including an extensive discussion of staff (characteristics, leadership criteria, education), care planning, and program areas (134 pages).

Calkins, Margaret P., M. Arch, *Design for Dementia: Planning Environments for the Elderly and the Confused.* Owings Mills, Md.: National Health Publishing, 1988.

This text focuses on understanding the problems of serving those with AD and designing the solution, offering specific modifications and low-cost solutions (185 pages). It is available from National Health Publishing for $36—for address, see Sources, below.

Freeman, Sally, *Activities and Approaches for Alzheimer's.* Knoxville, Tenn.: Whitfield Agency, 1987.

This is a useful resource for small group activities that offer maximum involvement and success and minimum frustration and failure (106 pages).

French, Carolyn, J. A. Coye, M. L. Dykes, and R. Ricketts, *Manual for Providers of In-Home Respite Care of Persons with Alzheimer's Disease.* Atlanta, Ga.: Atlanta Area Chapter, Alzheimer's Association, 1989.

Based upon a successful model respite program, this manual includes descriptions of respite services, a methodology for determining numbers of likely clients, and methods of reaching providers and potential users (more than 100 pages, including sample forms and documents and a copy of a Guide to Home Safety). It is available for $50 from the Atlanta Area Chapter, Alzheimer's Association, 3120 Raymond Drive, Atlanta, Georgia 30340, (404) 451-1300.

Gwyther, Lisa P. A.C.S.W., *Care of Alzheimer's Patients—A Manual for Nursing Home Staff.* Chicago, Ill.: Alzheimer's Association, 1985.

Designed for nursing home staff but also useful for staff of day centers—the manual clearly explains AD and its effects. It offers vignettes on particular behaviors with appropriate responses for staff, for families, for the facility and includes activities programming (122 pages). Prepared as a joint venture of the Alzheimer's Association and the American Health Care Association (AHCA), it is available for $6.95 from the national office of the Alzheimer's Association—for address, see Sources, below.

Hunter, Carlita, *Gray Hair and I Don't Care.* Harrisburg, N.C.: Hunter House Publications, 1990.

Designed for residents of nursing homes and adult day care centers, this book deals with everyday living and social skills (119 pages).

Levine, Gloria, R.N., B.S.N. and J. Scharf, A.C.S.W., L.I.S.W., *Serving Persons with Alzheimer's Disease: Training Manual* and *Managing Problem Behaviors of Persons with Alzheimer's* (Video Tape and Instructor's Guide). Columbus, Ohio: Ohio Association of Adult Day Care, 1987.

Designed for staff, students and volunteers in day centers, this video focuses on the nine most common particular behaviors associated with AD. It defines each behavior, discusses causes, and demonstrates proper intervention and prevention techniques. The guide accompanies the video as a training tool. The manual is designed to help center staff better serve persons with AD and includes goals, design, techniques, and activities (64 pages). All are available from the Ohio Association as a package for $55 or separately ($50 for the tape and guide and $15 for the manual)—for address, see Sources, below.

Mace, Nancy L, and P.V. Rabins, M.D., *The 36-Hour Day: A Family Guide to Caring for Persons with Alzheimer's Disease, Related Dementing Illnesses, and Memory Loss in Later Life.* Baltimore, Md.: The Johns Hopkins University Press, 1981.

A readable and useful description of AD, its progression, and its impact upon the individual and the family/caregiver, this volume offers practical and specific advice. It could be used as background for staff unfamiliar with AD (253 pages).

Nissenboim, Sylvia and C. Vroman, *Interaction by Design.* St. Louis, Mo.: Geri-Active Consultants, 1989.

This book offers a positive interaction program of individualized activities for participants with AD. It focuses on success for the participant and spending quality time together (103 pages).

Panella, John, Jr., M.A., M.P.H., *Day Care Programs for Alzheimer's Disease and Related Disorders.* New York, N.Y.: Demos Publications, 1987.

Specifically written to examine adult day care for those with AD, this book offers proven program ideas and management techniques. Its detailed and practical suggestions cover all major aspects of day center planning and operations (132 pages).

Sheridan, Carmel, M.A., *Failure-Free Activities for the Alzheimer's Patient.* Oakland, Calif.: Cottage Books, 1987.

Instructions on carrying out specific activities with the person with AD are presented simply and in detail. Intended primarily for caregivers, it also offers activities appropriate for day centers (104 pages). It may be available from local chapter of Alzheimer's Association.

Sincox, Rochelle B., O.T.R., and P.S. Cohen, *Adapting the Adult Day Care Environment for the Demented Older Adult.* Springfield, Ill.: The Illinois Department on Aging, 1986.

With background on AD and resulting behavior and adult day care, this offers specific instructions, preparations and materials for activities—identified by specific goals. Included are scales and descriptions of assessment processes for behavior and cognitive function (66 pages).

Vermeersch, Patricia E. Hadley, Ph.D., R.N., R. Greene and H. Meade, *Managing the Client With Dementia: A Resource and Training Guide for Nursing Homes and Adult Day Care Centers.* Trenton, N.J.: New Jersey Department of Health, 1988.

This is a training manual designed for trainers of direct care providers in nursing homes and day centers to convey information necessary in working with the adult with dementia. It also introduces management techniques in its eleven modules. Designed for use with professional staff, each module contains an Instructor's Guide, Lesson Plan, Handout, and Test (275 pages). Available for $15 from the Gerontology Program, Division of Epidemiology, New Jersey State Department of Health, 3635 Quakerbridge Road, CN 360, Trenton, NJ 08625.

Zgola, Jitka M., *Doing Things: A Guide to Programming Activities for Persons with Alzheimer's Disease and Related Disorders.* Baltimore, Md.: The Johns Hopkins University Press, 1987.

A thorough presentation of the challenges of programming for the individual with AD, this includes a sample schedule, activities (with instructions), and practical suggestions on interactions with participants (149 pages). It may be available from local chapter of the Alzheimer's Association.

Sources

ALZHEIMER'S ASSOCIATION
70 East Lake Street
Chicago, Illinois 60601
(312) 853-3060
Also, (800) 621-0379 for Information and Referral
In Illinois, (800)572-6037

NATIONAL HEALTH PUBLISHING
A Division of Williams and Wilkins
99 Painters Mill Road
Owings Mills, Maryland 21117-0990
(800) 638-0672

OHIO ASSOCIATION OF ADULT DAYCARE
36 West Gay Street
Columbus, Ohio 43215
(614) 221-2882

Glossary

activities of daily living (ADLs) - functions or tasks for self-care usually performed in the normal course of a day, including bathing, dressing, toileting, transferring, and eating plus mobility.

acuity - measurement of an individual's degree of impairment indicating the amount of care needed; the higher the acuity, the more intense the service.

adult day care - the full range of services provided to adults with functional impairments in a structured, supervised setting for less than 24 hours a day.

assistive listening devices - instruments used to improve the ability to hear (including mechanisms such as audioloops and microphones equipped with infrared devices).

audioloop - system of amplifying or magnifying sound within a defined area, linking into individual hearing aids.

care management - a component of the community care system: a process of managment which includes assessing the individual's functional level and impairments, developing a plan of care, identifying and arranging for coordinated delivery of services, monitoring changes, and periodically reassessing needs.

certification - the process in which an individual, an institution, or an educational program is evaluated and recognized as meeting certain predetermined standards deemed necessary for safe and ethical practice of the profession or service.

cognitive impairment - a weakening or deterioration of the mental processes of perception, memory, judgment, and reasoning.

counseling - an interactive process, on a one-to-one or group basis, in which an individual is provided guidance and assistance in the utilization of services and help in coping with personal problems through the establishment of a supportive relationship.

functional impairment - the limitation of an individual's functional ability, the inability to perform personal and instrumental activities of daily living and associated tasks, or the inability to establish and maintain an independent living arrangement.

holistic - treating the person as a whole—with recognition of his or her mental, physical, emotional, social, and spiritual aspects—while acknowledging his or her relationship to the broader systems of family and community.

individual plan of care - a written plan of services designed to provide the participant with appropriate services and treatment in accordance with his or her assessed needs.

in-kind contribution - payment made or given in goods, commodities, space, services, or time rather than money.

instrumental activities of daily living (IADLs) - functions or tasks of independent living, including shopping, housework, meal preparation and cleanup, laundry, taking medication, money management, transportation, correspondence, telephoning, and related tasks.

interdisciplinary team (or multi-disciplinary team) - all staff members responsible for the care of each participant who, together, assess the participant, make recommendations on interventions and services to be offered, and provide direct services.

long-term care - a coordinated continuum of preventive, diagnostic, therapeutic, rehabilitative, supportive, and maintenance services that address the health, social, and personal needs of individuals who have restricted self-care capabilities.

maintenance therapy - the preservation of strength or well-being achieved through remedial, rehabilitating, or curative processes.

NICLC - the National Institute on Community-based Long-term Care, a constituent unit of The National Council on the Aging, Inc.

paraprofessional - a person trained to assist a professional but not licensed to practice in the profession.

personal care - care provided to assist an individual with his/her ADL's.

physician, staff - a physician employed by the adult day care center.

psycho-social - involving both psychological and social aspects.

quality assurance - any evaluation of services provided and result achieved that is made in comparison to accepted standards.

respite - short-term, intermittent, substitute care provided in the absence of the regular caregiver provided for a person with impairments.

restorative or rehabilitative services - services intended to restore the individual to his/her optimal level of functioning.

strategic plan - plan, method, or series of strategies for obtaining specific goals or results, usually on a multi-year basis.

therapeutic - describes services and/or activities intended to be beneficial and related to treatment or to the plan of care.

unit dose - a pre-measured amount of medication.

Universal Precautions - infection control guidelines developed by the Centers for Disease Control, intended to protect the worker against possible HIV transmission through exposure to blood and certain other body fluids.